*Saradell Ard
Please return*

Portrait Masks from the Northwest Coast of America

J.C.H. King

W9-BWB-166

THAMES AND HUDSON

The illustration on the cover is of a Kwakiutl mask

Any copy of this book issued by the publisher as a paperback is
sold subject to the condition that it shall not, by way of trade or
otherwise, be lent, re-sold, hired out or otherwise circulated,
without the publisher's prior consent, in any form of binding or
cover other than that in which it is published, and without a
similar condition including these words being imposed on a
subsequent purchaser.

First published in the UK in 1979 by
Thames and Hudson Ltd, London

© Blacker Calmann Cooper Ltd, 1979
This book was designed and produced by
Blacker Calmann Cooper Ltd, London

All rights reserved. No part of this publication may be reproduced or transmitted in any form or by any means, electronic or
mechanical, including photocopy, recording or any information
storage and retrieval system, without permission in writing from
the publishers.

Filmset by Southern Positives and Negatives (SPAN), Lingfield,
Surrey
Printed in Spain by Heraclio Fournier, S.A.

Contents

Introduction · 5

Kwakiutl Masks 33

Nootkan Masks 43

Haida Masks 51

Tsimshian Masks 77

Tlingit Masks 83

Notes 94
Bibliography 94
Acknowledgements and list of illustrations 94
Index 96

Introduction

The masks of the indigenous peoples of the Northwest Coast of America are among the most remarkable artistic creations of any tribal society: they struck the first Europeans who saw them with the same compelling power that impresses us today. Although the early explorers were amazed by what they found, and collected huge numbers of Indian artifacts — tools, weapons, fishing equipment, carved and painted bowls, spoons, house posts and crest poles — they were particularly taken with human face masks both for their realism and their craftsmanship. The finest examples were collected in the hundred years before 1870 by people with only a superficial interest in the cultures of the Northwest Coast; so today we have very little detailed information about their use or symbolism. Very few of these masks survive; there may be only several hundred in existence out of a total of tens of thousands of Northwest Coast objects in collections round the world.

Although the masks discussed in this book are generally given the title of portrait masks, there is in fact only limited evidence of portraiture. As we know it, portraiture is a European concept developed from traditions which had little or no meaning in Indian society. A portrait is a work of art designed to stand on its own outside any ceremonial or ritual context. On the Northwest Coast everything had its explicit context and place and masks were carved for three specific occasions. The first was the representation of chiefs and ancestors of high rank; the second was the performance of dances re-enacting myths; the third was shamanism and healing. In all these contexts masks were used to highly dramatic effect. They were worn generally in winter and at night; the house where the feast was taking place would be filled with people and lit only by firelight in the centre. The atmosphere would be both tense and expectant of the drama to come. In these circumstances the use of portraiture was totally different from that in Europe. Representations of familiar spirits or ancestors were undoubtedly given certain life-like characteristics; more often masks projected forceful images of reality and imagination which expressed and emphasized the social and religious values of Northwest Coast society. In general, Indian artists were given few occasions to record the appearance of actual individuals.

The American and European travellers, explorers and missionaries who collected early artifacts looked at Indian art, together with Indian economic and political life, from a European point of view. The objects which were most praised were often masks representing the human form. When in the first half of the nineteenth century artifacts began to be made for sale, portrait masks may have been carved because realistic sculpture was what

1. Haida village of Skidegate. This photograph, like plate 17, was taken by Edward Dossetter, and shows a row of houses and poles carved with crests along the beach. *Late 19th Century. New York, American Museum of Natural History: negative 42267*

appealed most to the trader or traveller.

In spite of a considerable revival of interest, our knowledge is still very elementary and most of what is said about human face masks remains conjectural. We can be sure, however, that the people who made and used them valued them not only for their aesthetic qualities but for the essential part they played in the drama of their lives — the theatrical expression of their beliefs and the understanding of their existence. These marvellous creations provide a source of inspiration both for modern Indian artists and for those who are trying to understand something of the complex art and culture of the Northwest Coast before the arrival of Europeans. The artistic tradition of the Northwest Coast depended on implicit assumptions which are unlikely to have been stated or discussed even in Indian society. Artists learnt to carve by watching and copying their mentors; they were not taught in ways dependent on the use of words or concepts which could be easily articulated. Today the majority of Indian artists' work belongs to a mixed European and Indian tradition and is recognized as a major art form the world over.

Subsistence and Economy

This book discusses in detail the masks of five groups of the Northwest Coast — the Tlingit, Haida, Tsimshian, Kwakiutl and Nootka — living along part of a thousand-mile stretch of coastline from the Columbia River in the state of Washington to Yakutat Bay in Alaska. In the far north, in Alaska, live the Tlingit and one of the sub-tribes of the Haida. The great majority of the Haida live on the Queen Charlotte's Islands in British Columbia, and the Tsimshian, Kwakiutl and Nootka live along the coast, inlets, rivers and islands of British Columbia.

The geography of this huge area varies considerably; in the north the coast is pierced with deep inlets and surrounded by high mountains, and in the south it is fringed with hills through which broad rivers run. The climate is temperate, even in the north where the effects of the Japan Current are confined to a coastal belt separated from the sub-Arctic interior by high mountains. Throughout the region the sea, rivers and warm waters have always provided the inhabitants with an almost limitless supply of food, the primary source being five species of highly nutritious salmon which fill the rivers in profusion every year. Of the many other fish which made up the traditional Indian catch, the most important were halibut, herring, cod and eulachon, also called candlefish because its high oil content meant that, when dried and threaded with a wick, it could be used as a candle. Apart from

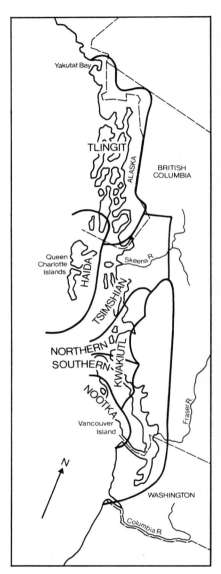

Map of the Northwest coast of America showing tribal areas.

2. **Haida or Northern Kwakiutl human face mask. The agonized expression suggests that it represents a spirit helper to a shaman or chief.** *c. 1825–75. Height 9¾in (25cm). Belfast, Ulster Museum: 103:1952*

molluscs gathered everywhere on the coast — it was said of them that 'when the tide goes out, the table is set' — the sea supplied other, though less regular, elements of diet. These included sturgeon speared on the Columbia River and whales, hunted only by the Nootka of Vancouver Island and the Makah, a related group,

of Washington State. On land berries were gathered in season, and animals such as the mountain goat were hunted for their wool and horn.

The main resources of the land, however, were the enormous trees and forests whose growth was fostered by the same damp warm climate which made the area so rich in food. Sitka spruce, red and yellow cedar, alder and hemlock spruce were used not only for building large communal houses, whaling and hunting canoes and ceremonial equipment, but also for clothing. Cedar bark was shredded and woven into cloaks and capes and worn as an alternative to skins.

Although the environment was extremely favourable, a fairly advanced technology was needed to exploit and preserve these many resources. Salmon, the staple food, were caught in traps and at weirs and speared in many different ways. Cod were lured to the surface and then speared; halibut were caught on two types of wooden hook, one carved, the other steamed and bent into shape. Herring appeared in such large quantities in spring that they were lifted from the water on the spiked blades of herring rakes. These techniques were refined and developed over several thousand years, enabling a dense population to subsist entirely by hunting and gathering. These circumstances, which in the past attracted peoples of very diverse origins into the area, also provided the conditions under which it was possible to evolve a sophisticated art style which became more or less common to the whole area. Elsewhere other hunting and gathering societies had to move around — to catch game or fish or to harvest wild plants as they came into season. In the plains of North America, for example, Indians had to travel hundreds of miles to follow the bison. In contrast, the peoples of the Northwest Coast were able to remain to an unusual extent in a single place. The leisure afforded by the seasonal and almost sedentary nature of their subsistence activities enabled them to spend time creating, carving and decorating ceremonial paraphernalia, houses and canoes which were without parallel among other such tribes.

Society and Religion

The Northwest Coast peoples, although belonging to different linguistic groups and coming from very different backgrounds, produced through time a common culture. Each tribe came with its own language, social system and material culture, but through the transference, adaptation and adoption of each other's ideas there gradually arose a common basis for their economic and ceremonial life. The social and political organization of Northwest

3. The inside of a house in Nootka Sound. This engraving shows many features of domestic life on the Northwest Coast. The central figures are sitting round a fire on which fish are being baked; other fish are being dried in the rafters, and the two kerfed and bentwood boxes probably contain food. All the people are wearing cedar bark capes and cloaks. This engraving was made by W. Sharp after a finished watercolour of 1778 by John Webber.

4. Tlingit mask of a woman wearing a labret. The facial painting above the left eyebrow and emerging from the left-hand side of the mouth depicts the killer whale's dorsal fin. The mask shows no sign of use and may, therefore, have been made for sale. This mask, with those illustrated in plates 10 and 95, were all sold by E. G. Fast to the Peabody Museum in the late 1860s. *c. 1860–65. Height 9in (23cm). Cambridge, Mass., Peabody Museum (Harvard University): 977-30-10/58192*

5. Tlingit shaman's mask. The hair, eyebrows and moustache on this mask were made from fur and nailed into place; it has copper eyes and lips. Although the face is extremely realistic, it probably represents a spirit who would have helped the shaman cure the sick and predict events. It was held to the wearer's head with a hide strap. Collected by J. G. Swan at Sitka, Alaska. *c. 1850–75. Height 12⅝in (32cm). Washington DC, Smithsonian Institution: 18929*

Coast society was, however, extremely diverse and complicated. The variations were most evident between the most northern and most southern tribes. Descent was the basic principle underlying all social and political organizations. The northern tribes, the Tlingit, Tsimshian and Haida, were all matrilineal – that is, descent was traced through the female line so that a man inherited wealth and social position from his mother's brother. Among the southern tribes, the Nootka and Southern Kwakiutl, descent was bilateral and could be traced either through the male or female line, although there was a slight preference for patrilineal descent.

In the north the more rigid system of matrilineal descent brought about the organization of *lineages*. Lineages were groups of people who traced their descent from a common ancestor, lived in one geographical area and held property in common. Often this meant that a single village would consist of all the members of one lineage. In the south a village was made up of a series of extended families without their necessarily sharing the bond of common descent. Everywhere on the Northwest Coast the inhabitants of a village might number a few hundred people and divide their year between a sheltered winter village site and a summer village base

6. Medicine Mask Dance. A painting by Paul Kane of an imaginary shaman's ritual with Indians wearing masks which he had previously seen at Fort Victoria on Vancouver Island. This painting, executed in 1847, is typical of illustrations of Northwest Coast life in the nineteenth century; people and artifacts were sketched separately, as here, and then integrated into a finished oil painting or watercolour. *Toronto, Royal Ontario Museum: 912.1.92*

for fishing. Villages and lineages were led by chiefs who owed their position to their inherited status and wealth. It was chiefs who owned rights to salmon weirs, beaches and areas where berries were gathered. They controlled access and determined relations, both ceremonial and economic, with neighbouring villages and tribes.

There were two other social organizations in the north which provided a web of social relationships spreading across the boundaries between villages and tribes. These were also founded on the principle of matrilineal descent from a common ancestor, either real or mythological. They are known as *moieties* and *clans*. The Haida, for instance, were divided into two moieties (a moiety meaning literally a half), to which everyone in all the lineages belonged; one was called the Eagles and the other the Ravens. Membership of, for instance, the Raven moiety was inherited from the mother, and meant that a person belonged to the same moiety as his/her brothers and sisters and sisters' children. The Tlingit were organized into clans as well as moieties. The importance of these moieties and clans was that people were forbidden to marry members of the same moiety or of the same clan; this meant that they had a unifying effect on society as a whole.

For the Tlingit, Tsimshian and Haida, lineages, clans and moieties, all with their own myths of origin, provided members with crests and other symbols of individual and group membership. According to a Tlingit myth explaining how animal crests were acquired, there was a time when everybody lived in darkness in a village at the mouth of the Nass River. The sun, moon and stars were kept in a box by the supreme deity who was called Raven-at-the-Mouth-of-the-Nass-River. His sister had a child, who was also a raven, to whom nobody showed any respect, even though he said that he could give them daylight. So he let the sun out of the box and it ascended into the sky with such a roar that many people were frightened out of the village and into the forests and water. As they were wearing furs at the time, they turned into the animals of the furs which clothed them. The people who remained in the village adopted the animals as crests in remembrance of their relations. The most common animal crests in the north included the frog, raven and killer whale, but there was also a large number of other crests, many of which represented creatures with no counterparts in the real world.

There were no highly developed or systematic concepts of deities, creation or religion; just as the various tribes had diverse myths to explain the origin of their crests, so they looked up to different supreme deities and spirits whom they regarded as their patrons or guardians. Among the Kwakiutl the supreme deities were sometimes, although not always, connected with the sun. The Nootka recognized four great chiefs, each of whom ruled part of the universe. The sky and the supernatural world were interpreted in widely differing ways. Most Haida, for example, thought of the sky as being in the form of an inverted bowl with spirits or supernatural beings on top. One lineage saw it as a series of five layers or levels, one on top of the other, its four upper levels being important in different contexts. The supreme deity of the upper world was Power-of-the-Shining-Heavens; it was to him that people prayed in sorrow or fear, and it was he who decided when people would die. Of the land spirits the most important was the Sacred-One-Standing-and-Moving. It was he who supported the Queen Charlotte's Islands: when there was an earthquake he moved, and it was to him that people prayed, 'Upon your good land let me live long'. The sea spirits included fish and sea mammals who lived in houses, like mortals. Ritually the most important of these was the killer whale, the only marine species which there was a supernatural dread of killing. Finally there were patron spirits who helped their mortal equivalents in the world as, for instance, the Master Carver who was able to build a house in a day.

In general patron spirits were of many different kinds, although most were associated through the inheritance of crests with a particular lineage or family. Spirits also provided the shaman with his powers of healing and prediction. A shaman's powers were both inherited (amongst the Haida from a maternal uncle) and acquired by contact with or possession by a spirit. In his lifetime a shaman would accumulate more powers, which he would pass on to his heir before his death. It was the duty of a shaman to cure those who had become bewitched by their enemies by revealing to the sick the identity of the enemy. For their services shamans were paid, for instance, with slaves. Their other functions included foretelling when whales would be cast ashore and accompanying war parties to predict the best time to attack.

Shamanism was important throughout the Northwest Coast, as were the myths associated with food-producing animals who were believed to be immortal. Salmon, for instance, appeared each year off-shore, went upstream, spawned and died. At death they returned to the salmon house under the sea as people. In reality, therefore, it was thought that if the bones of the salmon were returned to the water, the return of the salmon the following year would be ensured. In this connection preparatory rituals before fishing were very important. On the other hand it was usually only animals of little or no significance to the economy, such as the

7. Haida figure of a shaman, from a grave. This is the first of a series of figures said to represent a shaman who fell down in the woods, broke his legs and starved to death. If it does represent a real person, it is one of the earliest known Haida portraits. *c. 1825–50. Height 21½in (55cm). London, British Museum: 1944 Am 2 131*

8. Northern Kwakiutl mask, possibly representing a non-human character called Bookwus, or Wild-Man-of-the-Woods. He has been given distorted features, particularly a projecting mouth. *c. 1850–60. Height 10⅜in (26·5cm). London, British Museum: 1944 Am 2 NN*

9. Interior of a Kwakiutl house before a potlatch. This early photograph shows trade blankets piled up awaiting distribution, or perhaps destruction, at a feast symbolizing the wealth and power of a chief. *c. 1900. New York, American Museum of Natural History: negative 22861*

raven, killer whale and octopus, that were important as crests and as spirit helpers.

Mythological and religious ideas were given their fullest expression at feasts held by chiefs, although the extent to which these occasions were held to be sacred varied considerably. At potlatches, as these feasts are called, chiefs presented their heirs and relations and bestowed upon them ancestral rights. Enormous quantities of food were provided for the invited relations and guests and other gifts, such as blankets, were also given away. In accepting these things, the guests could be said to have accepted, for instance, the chief's relative as heir and the rights and obligations that this implied. Potlatches impressed upon the audience, as well as upon the participants, the fundamental principles of social status and organization and the relationship of society to the supernatural world on which it depended. This was because religion was not something which could be separated from other aspects of social life, but was an essential part of it and was manifested in many different activities, including these feasts. Although the nature and ceremonial content of potlatches varied from tribe to tribe, there were two important elements: first, as mentioned above, particularly amongst the northern tribes, the passing on of property, status and honour from a chief to his heir; secondly, particularly amongst the peoples of southern British Columbia, initiation into and participation in what are usually described as secret or dancing 'societies'. These societies are, perhaps, better thought of as groups of people (organized in a

10. Tlingit shaman's mask in the form of a bear. Northwest Coast carvings of bears, and all mammals, often resemble human beings. Only the long animal-like nose and the ears on top rather than at the side distinguish it as a bear. The three small figures emerging from the cheeks and top of the head may be bear cubs – additional spirit helpers to the shaman. *c. 1840–60. Height $10\frac{5}{8}$ in (27cm). Cambridge, Mass., Peabody Museum (Harvard University): 69-30-10/1609*

hierarchical structure) who performed dances re-enacting myths. They were also the means by which inherited privileges were handed down and children and adolescents were introduced to a full understanding of tribal life. Among the most northern tribes the potlatch was more explicitly concerned with the family of the host. For instance, a succession of Tlingit feasts was given over a period of years to mourn the death of a chief: the first would be an expression of thanks to those who had actually carried out the funerary rites, another would be to erect a mortuary column, or pole, carved with the crests of the dead man. With the Tsimshian the emphasis was not on the mourning of the chief, but on the inheritance of property by his heir. The Haida attached importance to the establishment of the potential heir as the man who would inherit a chief's position and possessions; as befitted a matrilineal society, an important Haida feast took place when a son left his father's home to go and live with the maternal uncle whom he would eventually succeed as chief. At this potlatch he would be honoured by his father.

11. **Tsimshian chiefs with heirlooms. Chiefs were most usually posed alongside, rather than using, masks and other ceremonial artifacts. This photograph includes a number of human — and possibly portrait — masks in the foreground.** *Prince Rupert. Museum of Northern British Columbia*

History of the Northwest Coast

From the first substantial exploration of the Northwest Coast in the 1770s, first by the Spanish and then by the British, the Indian peoples' way of life and their art were first transformed and subsequently, over the next hundred years, radically reduced by European contact and colonization. What we know of Indian art today must, therefore, be understood in this historical perspective.

Captain James Cook's visit to the Northwest Coast in 1778 provided the first reason for the exploration and the colonization of the area: the discovery of the wealth of valuable sea-otter pelts used as clothing amongst the Nootka. In the following year the expedition was able to sell pelts in China, which had been obtained for a few nails, glass beads or pieces of copper, for up to $120 each. On Cook's return to England commercial interests financed the fitting out of more ships to pursue this lucrative trade. This initial period of contact with the peoples of the Northwest Coast lasted until the 1820s and was dominated by New England traders. The fiercest political rivalry was between the Spanish and the British in the south, leading to Spanish withdrawal during the 1790s. In the north the Russians dominated the fur trade and established trading forts such as the one at Sitka among the Tlingit. The influence of European trade and technology at this time was relatively limited. Iron, already used in small but significant quantities on the Northwest Coast in the 1770s, became a common commodity — as did copper, a metal which was used for sheathing the hulls of wooden vessels and which possessed a ritual and ceremonial significance in Indian society. Besides these metals many other foreign goods were traded to the Indians, and many of them became incorporated into their culture. For instance, Cook saw and purchased two silver Spanish spoons which were being worn as decoration round the neck. A more substantial change came with the trading of coarse blue woollen cloth which began to supersede, particularly in the south, Indian clothing of animal skins and cedar bark decorated with dog's and goat's wool.

It is more difficult to pinpoint precise changes in technology and material culture brought about by the increased acquisition of metals, but it obviously became easier to create larger and more extravagant houses and ritual and ceremonial paraphernalia. Weapons changed much faster, the Spaniards probably being the first to trade muskets to the Indians; iron knives became common and aboriginal weapons became obsolete. The Nootkan club, which Cook called a 'tomahawk', disappeared at the beginning of the nineteenth century. This club was carved with the head of a man and the striking blade consisted of an enormous stone tongue

12. Haida mask of a dead man (?). The deathly and grotesque expression is produced by the deep stylized carving of the eye sockets and cheeks. This results in sharply conflicting planes defined by swirling lines around the eyes and cheek bones. As in many Kwakiutl masks, the definition of the eyes as arcs, rather than modified ovals, strengthens its impact. *c. 1885. Height 13in (33cm). Berlin, Museum für Völkerkunde: 1V A 6781*

13. Haida mask of a woman wearing a labret. This is the finest of a series of masks (plates 46, 47, 50, 51, 52, 53, 56, 57, 58) all carved by one artist. They almost all represent a woman wearing a labret, and have the same realistic, if simplified, features. It is likely that they are Haida rather than Tlingit or Tsimshian because the carving of the eyes and the cross-hatching is characteristically Haida. These masks probably represent an ancestor, the abstract formlines on them being crests. It was collected by Captain Daniel Cross in 1827. *c. 1827. Height 10¼in (26cm). Salem, Peabody Museum: E 3483*

set into the face. The Tlingit, as a result of Russian weapons, rapidly abandoned their wooden armour and war helmets (plate 19), although the latter may still have been used ceremonially.

As the sea otter was pursued almost to extinction by Indians for trade to Americans and Europeans, the centre of the fur trade shifted. Nootka Sound, the original centre, was by the nineteenth century a refuge for ships rather than a place of trade. When Europeans began to look for alternative furs to sell, the indigenous peoples changed their hunting and trading patterns to provide them. The supply of these furs came from the mainland and largely from land rather than sea animals. The first trading fort to be established in the south was Fort Astoria, set up by the American Pacific Fur Company on the Columbia River in 1811. Thorough exploitation of the fur resources of the coast began only with the amalgamation of two British companies, the North West Company and the Hudson's Bay Company, in 1821.

With the presence of these forts the effect of European contact and colonization brought in its wake much more fundamental changes than those already discussed; it was responsible for the introduction of new diseases and a rapid decline in the indigenous population which had disastrous consequences for the Indian way of life and culture. Also relations between Indians and Europeans gradually changed and the mutually beneficial trading of the earlier period ended. In the beginning massacres were committed on both sides, but an uneasy truce was brought about by the Europeans in order to keep the friendship of chiefs from whom sea otter pelts were obtained. Later in the nineteenth century, after the murder of white men, whole villages were destroyed in order to maintain the authority of the Hudson's Bay Company. With the arrival of guns, wars between Indians became much more destructive and savage; in some places those tribes first to obtain guns were able to drive out and destroy their enemy neighbours.

In the nineteenth century venereal disease arrived on the Northwest Coast as an inevitable result of the fur trade. But this was not as disastrous as the advent of smallpox in the 1780s and 1790s, which in 1836 spread southwards, completely decimating the Indian population. It has been estimated that, before the arrival of Europeans, there were about 8,000 Haida. By the 1830s the numbers had dropped to about 6,700, and after the effects of smallpox in the 1880s to only 800. Although the figures varied from one tribe to another, the overall effects on Indian institutions and culture were the same. As populations declined, access to wealth became easier for those not of high birth. This happened, although there were fewer people, because food, resources,

14. **Portrait bust of Captain George Reid, RN. A Tlingit Indian at Fort Rupert is said to have carved this bust in 1860; it demonstrates the artist's remarkable ability to carve realistically, and was almost certainly made for trade.** *c. 1860. Height 3¾in (9·5cm). London, British Museum: 7764*

ceremonial privileges and artifacts were unaffected and existed in the same quantities. Whereas originally chiefs had controlled trade and access to wealth, now all Indians could trade on their own account, and also engage in paid labour at the forts and towns of the settlers. Among the Kwakiutl of Fort Rupert, where rivalry between chiefs and high-ranking individuals was very fierce, a category of *nouveau riche* men was given the title of 'Eagles'; they were not allowed to assume traditional crests or names, but their anomalous position — the challenge of their wealth to the traditional authority of chiefs — was formalized in this way.

The colonization of the Northwest Coast brought wealth, but it also brought a direct assault on the ideas fundamental to Indian society. Feasts and potlatches called for the acquisition of enormous amounts of 'capital' in the form of trade blankets and quantities of food; this was dispersed by being consumed, given away or destroyed to enhance the authority of the host. None of these resources was invested in the European sense, and so they were a direct challenge to the Protestant ethic of the colonists with its idea of the productive investment of capital. A further clash arose over apparent cannibalism; the performances of the secret societies contained references and detailed re-enactions of myths describing the consumption of human flesh by mythical beings.

Attempts were, therefore, made from the 1880s onwards to eliminate the potlatch. The climax of the campaign took place in 1921 when large amounts of ritual paraphernalia were seized by the police at the Kwakiutl village of Alert Bay. This underlying hostility was fundamental to Indian-European relations and affected the circumstances in which the most important human face masks were collected.

A very large percentage of the surviving portrait masks was collected before 1870, and their carving and sale must be understood in the context of the rapid disintegration of Indian institutions at this time. Masks were collected in several different ways before 1870, and these activities determine what is known of their manufacture and significance. In the earliest period masks were traded, for instance, to Cook because the Nootka were anxious to obtain metal. They had probably not seen white people before, and so had no idea whether they would come back. The fur traders and whalers who followed exchanged copper, iron, blankets and later alcohol for Indian artifacts, as well as for furs and food — although some of the early traders placed severe restrictions on this type of collecting to ensure high prices, in terms of furs, for their trade goods. With the extension of trade it seems probable that

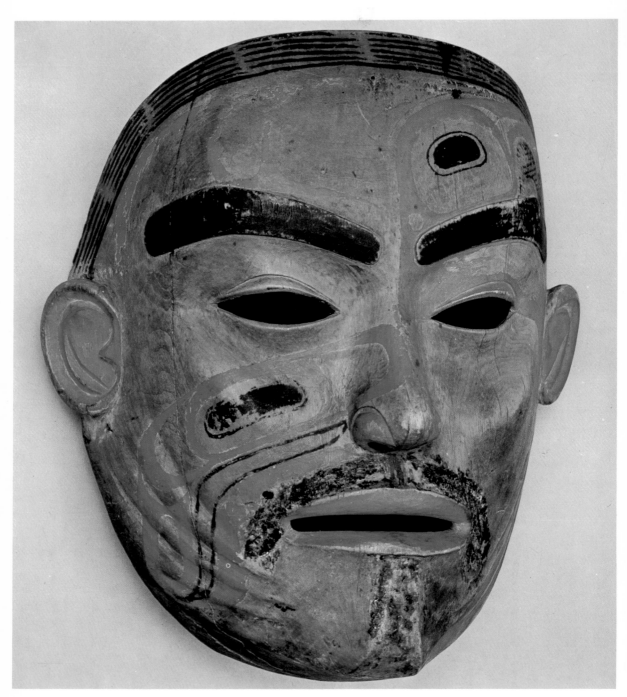

15. Haida mask of a man which, like those in plates 16 and
18, is painted with highly abstract formline designs probably
representing crests, and like plate 16, is carved with wrinkled
cheeks. The eyes vary considerably; this has the very
unusual feature of an incised line representing the upper
eyelid. It was collected in 1878 by George Dawson. *c. 1825–75.*
Height 10$\frac{1}{4}$in (26cm). Houston, de Menil Collection

16. Haida mask of a man. This, together with those masks in
plates 15 and 18, is perhaps the finest surviving Haida
human face mask. Although none was collected with any
definite documentation, they all probably represent Haida
chiefs painted with crests. This one has movable eyelids.
c. 1825–75. Height 10$\frac{1}{2}$in (27cm). London, British Museum:
1949 Am 22 62

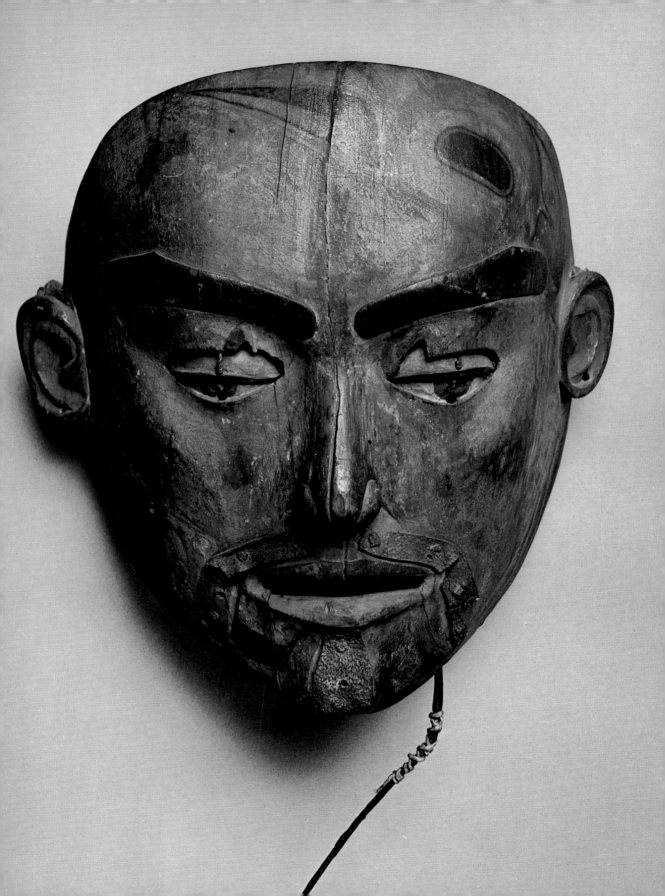

only ceremonially insignificant items were regularly traded to American and European sea captains. At this time souvenirs, such as wooden models of war or sea-otter hunting canoes, were already being made by the Haida and Nootka. No doubt important sea captains were still able to obtain, or were presented with, objects considered significant by the Indians.

In the nineteenth century with the decline of the sea-otter trade larger numbers of souvenirs were produced and were probably stocked in the fur company forts for sale to sailors, painters or other visitors to the Northwest Coast. The Canadian artist, Paul Kane, made sketches showing masks from a number of tribes at Fort Victoria in 1847; George Catlin perhaps acquired the human face masks for his London exhibition of the 1840s from a similar trading company source. Another sailor who was able to purchase masks on the Columbia River, 100 miles west of Fort Vancouver, was Lieutenant Charles Wilkes who led the United

17. Four Haida. Very few photographs exist of masks being worn; this illustrates three Haida wearing masks of human face form, and a fourth man with crest tattoos on his chest and arm. It was taken by Edward Dossetter in the nineteenth century at Masset on the Queen Charlotte Islands. *1881. New York, American Museum of Natural History: negative 42314*

States Exploring Expedition of 1838–42 (plates 49, 52, 53). Under those circumstances it is not surprising therefore that masks of this early period are poorly understood by anthropologists. It is this, and the sensitivity of the carving, which has given rise to the frequent claim that many of them are portraits. Franz Boas, the greatest anthropologist of the Northwest Coast, arrived in 1886 with photographs and drawings of masks whose significance he wanted to ascertain. He discovered that it was seldom possible to find the exact significance of individual masks unless he visited the villages from which they came. This was partly because masks were made for the use of particular individuals who gave them their meaning, and partly because masks were traded from village to village and tribe to tribe and in this process their meaning was liable to change or become lost.

Two other types of collecting began during the second half of the nineteenth century. Missionaries obtained large numbers of objects from those they were endeavouring to convert and these were sent, for instance, to England for display. Missionary museums and exhibitions stimulated interest and, thereby, money for the conversion of Indians, but the meaning of the masks was almost always irrelevant to the collectors' purposes. Anthropologists purchased, commissioned and removed Indian artifacts from the 1880s onwards to museums in eastern North America and Europe. These collections and the accompanying documentation provide the most useful information we have, since they were acquired from people who had actually used them.

The Art of the Northwest Coast

On the Northwest Coast artifacts were decorated in a distinctive style. The largest and most obvious examples are the carved and painted canoes, house fronts, house posts and crest poles, but the range extends from all forms of ceremonial paraphernalia to such utilitarian objects as fish-hooks. It was the masks, however, on which the greatest ingenuity, care and attention were lavished. Of the many different types it was those depicting the human face which were at once the simplest and the most sophisticated. They are simple because the subject-matter is straightforward, and because the technical skill of the carving is apparently uncompli-cated. Also the mechanical parts – for manipulating eyes, eyelids, jaws and lips – were relatively easy to make and to use. Many other masks were far larger – for instance, the bird masks used in the Kwakiutl Hamatsa dance were up to six feet long. Many of these larger masks had elaborate mechanisms so that, for example, an outer mask in the form of a wolf might open up at a dramatic moment in a dance to reveal the sun. The sophistication of human face masks lies in the understanding of the human form and the artist's ability to communicate this understanding in a variety of dramatic ways. Before these masks are described in detail, it is important to understand something of the principles underlying Northwest Coast art.

The general and the specific characteristics of Northwest Coast art have been the subject of considerable research over the last hundred years which has concentrated on four different aspects. First is the use of highly stylized symbols for different animals and mythological creatures; these are usually identified by certain standard features, such as the symbolical depiction of the dorsal fin of the killer whale in an otherwise abstract design of the mammal. The symbolism was first explained at the end of the nineteenth century by Franz Boas. Second is the repeated use of specific shapes, volumes, lines and colours so that each element of a particular design relates rhythmically and symmetrically to the whole. This means that in the carving of a pole or a mask the complete design with all its interrelated parts is conceived before work actually begins; the artist does not design the object experimentally as he proceeds. Third, the style of the painting and carving approaches realism, but it is a qualified realism. Reality is distorted so that the visual impact of an image arises from a single point or points in the exaggerated features of an animal mask. The important features of a carving, the eyes, nose and mouth, are brought out and expanded so that they dominate the whole object. This results in simplification, even when realism is the probable intention of the artist. These sculptural forms were studied by Paul Wingert during the 1940s. Finally, the most distinctive feature of Northwest Coast art is the use of highly abstract two-dimensional symbolical functions and meanings. These are painted and carved and are bilaterally symmetrical; on masks they represent animals, used as crests, whose features are split open and rearranged so that they appear on a single surface. All these designs are created from what are known as formlines, the name given to broad swelling and tapering lines which join and interlock to define the design. The basic outline is normally in black and is called the primary formline; the secondary formlines are usually red, and the final or tertiary formlines are normally painted in blue or green. The principles of these abstract designs were first described by Bill Holm relatively recently.

The semi-realism and the abstract surface designs are often combined: a wooden feast dish, for instance, might be carved in the form of a beaver with flat features painted and carved in low relief in this abstract style, but the face and tail would have three-

18. Haida mask of a man. Like plates 15 and 16, this was originally decorated with fur to represent a moustache and beard; the unusual feature is the combination of traditional formline designs with entirely abstract markings around the left eye. Unlike most early nineteenth-century Haida human face masks, this was evidently made for use; at some stage — perhaps before it was collected — it split open and was pinned together again. *c. 1800–50. Height 10½in (27cm). Washington DC, Smithsonian Institution: 73332B*

dimensional features. In bowls and objects the abstract designs may be partly recessed, but in masks they are always painted. Another unusual aspect of these abstract designs when used on masks is that they are rarely symmetrical. This decorative scheme was formalized by the northern tribes, the Tlingit, Haida and Tsimshian, but its origin probably lies in a little-known earlier art style common to the whole of the Northwest Coast. During the nineteenth century the Southern Kwakiutl, and to a much lesser extent the Nootka, began to adopt the intellectualized design principles of the north. Although it is simple to distinguish artifacts of southern British Columbia from those of the north, it is sometimes more difficult to attribute with any certainty a particular object decorated with these designs to the Haida, Tsimshian or Tlingit.

Variations in the sculpture and in the details of human face masks also help to define tribal origins. Southern masks are much more massive than those of the north, that is, they have heavy concentrated features making a strong visual impact; those of the north are more simply and more realistically carved. Masks everywhere were decorated with facial painting which was seldom delineated with incised lines. However, sculpted features such as the carving of the eye may be emphasized by a single incised line, although the Tsimshian seldom used this technique. Eyebrows are normally carved as slightly raised bands; Haida eyebrows, characteristically, have a more monumental effect with more substantial proportions. Tlingit masks and sculpture are carved with lips forming a single continuous band; Tsimshian and Haida lips are more often broken at the corners. Characteristics by which masks can be attributed to specific tribal origins, therefore, vary from mask to mask. With human face masks the problems of attribution are more difficult; as the carver inclined towards realism, and as the masks became more refined and like portraits, the tribal variations tended to disappear. Although it is relatively simple to distinguish masks from tribes not geographically contiguous, there is an area where the Haida, Tsimshian and Northern Kwakiutl meet in which the tribal variations are very confused as a result of trade and warfare. If it is difficult to identify the tribes from which the masks come, it is even more difficult to identify the person or spirit represented.

The depiction or representation of individuals, or particular categories of people such as ancestors or guardian spirits, was achieved by relatively few techniques. For instance, the carving and painting itself might portray individual physical characteristics, but how often this happened is impossible to determine since there

19. Tlingit war helmet. The carving of war helmets often included the same features as those reproduced in masks. Here the pursed lips are similar to those of singing shamans' masks (plates 89 and 90).
c. 1825–40. Height 8in (20·5cm). Leningrad, Museum of Anthropology and Ethnography: 571-17

20. Woman's labret or lip plug, inlaid with abalone shell. *c. 1825–75. Length 3in (7·5cm). London, British Museum: 1939 Am 11 2*

are no photographs or sketches of people whose masks have survived. However, the Haida artists' skill in copying European objects — such as steamboats, lions and sphinxes — suggests that this may have been a significant aspect of their art. The most common physical features depicted on masks are moustaches and facial hair on men and signs of age on women such as wrinkles. Another notable detail of the carving is the representation of facial decoration, including the piercing of the nose, ears and lips for the insertion of ornaments. The most common of these was the labret, or lip plug, worn by women of high rank. The status of the woman depended on the size of the labret in her lower lip; this was achieved gradually by inserting larger and larger ornaments into the original cut. Before the arrival of Europeans, girls on reaching puberty were traditionally considered ritually unclean, and so were secluded in separate dwellings. At the beginning of this seclusion the lower lip was pierced for the insertion of the first small labret. Once again, it is not clear whether variation in the size and decoration of labrets was a sign of individuality and therefore indicative of portraiture in masks, or whether it indicated general attributes such as a person's status or age.

Facial painting on masks usually represented designs of crests and shamans' spirits. Among the northern Northwest Coast Indians crests were inherited from real or mythological ancestors in the form of animals. A chief and his family would have a large number of crests, but only the chief would be entitled to use them all. Initially, young men were allowed to wear only the most general kind of crests, that is ones which were the property of groups rather than individuals. As they grew in status and position, so they were granted the privileges of using crests of higher status. For the Haida the more realistic the crest, the more prestigious it was. Most Tlingit human face masks are connected with shamanism rather than with crests and the painting symbolizes, in a very abstract way, an animal or other natural spirit helper. Further south, amongst the Kwakiutl, a smaller proportion of human masks were made and the painting on them represented characters in the performances of the winter dances. Facial painting, therefore, when transferred on to masks is another possible way in which portraiture and representation may have been realized.

Kwakiutl Masks

The ceremonial paraphernalia of the Kwakiutl is the most extensive and fantastic of all the peoples of the Northwest Coast. The hugely elaborate equipment is particularly associated with the dances performed in the course of feasts and potlatches by several different societies. Most of what is known of these comes from records made by observers of Southern Kwakiutl ceremonies in the late nineteenth and early twentieth centuries. The performances were held during the winter months when subsistence activities were at a minimum. This season which lasted from November onwards was called Tsetseka, meaning good-humoured or happy.

At the heart of the Tsetseka was the belief that during the winter months spirits, who in summer were thought to live elsewhere, came to the village to capture and abduct certain members. The dances and rituals were performed to reclaim those people. Generally these performances provided the occasion for the initiation of novices who were possessed by wild spirits and taken away to a place where they learnt of an ancestral right before being returned and re-established as full members of their group.

The most important ritual was performed by the Hamatsa dancers. It began with the disappearance of the novice into the woods, possessed by a spirit called Bakbakwalanooksiwae, meaning Cannibal-at-the-North-End-of-the-World, who inspired him with the desire to eat human flesh. Throughout the time of his absence, during which it was thought that he was being initiated into the ways of the cannibal spirit, and of his return and reclamation, dancers associated with the spirit appeared in masks. The most spectacular of these were the great bird monster masks representing mythical creatures who lived off human flesh. Another was the Thunderbird, which caused thunder by the beat of its wings and lightning by the flash of its eyes. It was so large that it caught whales in its talons.

Some of the Thunderbird's songs were recorded by Franz Boas, illustrating the Kwakiutl conception of these violent spirits:

You are swooping down from heaven, pouncing upon a
  whole tribe.
You are swooping down from heaven, burning villages,
  killing everything before you, and the remains of the
  tribes are like the rest of your food, great thunder bird:
  great thunderer of our world.
You are swooping down from heaven, going from one tribe
  to the other. You seize with your talons the chiefs of the
  tribes. (1)

Other masked dancers included the helpers or messengers of the Hamatsa, the Fool Dancer or Noohlmahl, whose role was also to

21. Tsimshian human face mask. An extraordinary feeling of pain and emotion is imparted by the careful modelling of the eyes and mouth and the abstract designs across the cheeks and forehead, suggesting that the mask is more likely to have been associated with a shaman than with a chief. It is thought to represent a Northern Kwakiutl (Bella Bella) spirit, and was collected by Lieutenant G. T. Emmons, perhaps the greatest collector of Northwest Coast artifacts in the late nineteenth and early twentieth centuries. c. 1875–1900. Height 12in (30·5cm). Houston, de Menil Collection

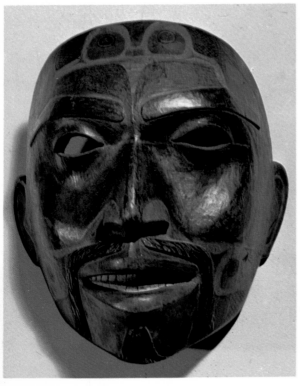

22. Northern Kwakiutl mask of a man. Although from the type of painting, the form of the eyes and the shape of the face, these masks appear to be Northern Kwakiutl, it is possible that they are Haida – and that the decorative details were borrowed from the Kwakiutl. None of this series (plates 22, 23, 24) is sufficiently well documented for its origin to be ascribed to an exact place or tribe. *c. 1825–75. Height 8½in (22cm). Ipswich, Museum: DLJ 28. 1976*

23. Northern Kwakiutl mask of a man which shows no sign of ever having been used. *c. 1825–75. Height 9¼in (23·5cm). London, British Museum: 1563*

keep the spectators under control. The masks of the Noohlmahl look like representations of the human face, but they are extremely distorted. One form of Noohlmahl mask apparently changed very little in the nineteenth century, so that of all early masks it is the one which can be most easily identified and placed in its context (plate 26). The Noohlmahl is a dirty creature with long matted hair which is represented in the masks by a carved mane framing the face. Even more important is the Noohlmahl's enormous nose which constantly runs with mucus; the nose on the masks is always shown as very large and rounded, with stylized mucus appearing from each nostril. When dancing the Noohlmahl is very sensitive about his appearance and particularly about his nose which he attempts to keep covered. Any reference to the nose or to smell makes him very angry and he strikes out at the audience with a club. One of his duties may have been to provide, symbolically or otherwise, human flesh for the Hamatsa to eat. Little is known of the extent to which people were killed or eaten, but by the late nineteenth century any cannibalism which might have

24. Northern Kwakiutl mask of a man. This is undoubtedly the finest of the three masks representing the same man or spirit which were carved by one artist in the middle of the nineteenth century. The painting, although not as complicated as that in plate 22, is more delicate than that on plate 23. *c. 1825–75. Height 8½in (22cm). Salem, Peabody Museum: E 28573*

25. Northern Kwakiutl human face mask. A heavily carved mask painted black, red and blue, of unknown significance. The eyes are not pierced so that the wearer would have looked through the nostrils. It was collected in the 1870s by J. G. Swan at Bella Bella, British Columbia. *c. 1850–75. Height 9in (23cm). Washington DC, Smithsonian Institution: 20578*

existed had disappeared and was only expressed symbolically. The madness of the Noohlmahl was calmed with songs describing his actions:

> Great is the fury of these supernatural ones.
> He will carry men away on his arms and torment them.
> He will devour them skin and bones, crushing flesh and bones
>   with his teeth.(2)

After the Hamatsa ritual the second most important dance was that featuring Winalagilis, meaning Warrior-of-the-World, a giant who travels around in a canoe which he never leaves. The many attendants of Winalagilis include ghosts who had the power to return the dead to life. Throughout these performances tricks enabled the dancers to achieve magical and enthralling effects. One of these concerned a character called Toogwid, who was usually portrayed as a woman. She dances while singers extol the supernatural qualities conferred on her by war. She taunts the audience to kill her by cutting open her stomach or beheading her. Eventually she sits down and one of her attendants does as she asks. In one performance an attendant drives a wedge through the dancer's head: a real wedge is shown to the audience while a false one is attached to the dancer's head so that it appears as though the real one has been driven through. Bladders of blood are burst to accompany the deed, including one in the dancer's mouth. To

26. Kwakiutl mask representing the spirit Noohlmahl. Noohlmahl was a fool dancer of revolting appearance. This interpretation gives him the form of a lion of European or American derivation – probably the figurehead of a sailing ship. The Kwakiutl artist has turned the mane into hair which was matted and unkempt; the lion's whiskers have become the mucus always flowing from Noohlmahl's nose. *c. 1825–75. Height 11¾in (29cm). Ipswich, Museum: 1948. 214.9*

27. Haida mask of a woman wearing a labret. The effect of carving the eyes as pierced arcs gives the mask an expression of pain. The idea may originate from a Northern Kwakiutl group, although it is also used in masks attributed to the Haida and Tsimshian. The labret in this mask was manipulated by means of a string so that the wearer could suggest lip movement. *c. 1850–1900. Height 9¼in (23·5cm). Houston, de Menil Collection*

28. Kwakiutl human face mask. This type of mask is characteristically Kwakiutl, but it is not known which character it would have represented in the winter dance performances. *c. 1825–75. Height 8½in (22cm). Ipswich, Museum: DLJ 30.1976*

give a greater realistic touch two seal's eyes are made to fall from the hair to represent the dancer's eyes — which have been forced out of their sockets. After dancing once around the house, all traces of the blow from the wedge disappear and she recovers completely. In another performance the dancer is burnt in a box, a trick achieved by hiding a skeleton in a double-bottomed coffin — the dancer escapes through a trapdoor; while the fire is burning the audience hears the dancer singing from the box — through a tube from the pit. In yet another performance the dancer is apparently beheaded and the audience sees a wood portrait carving of the dancer roll to the floor (plates 32, 33).

The masks and dances of these sacred rituals have few references to human beings and there are few occasions for the portrayal or representation of actual persons. However, many of the finest human face masks in existence today were acquired from the Northern Kwakiutl in the early nineteenth century. Some of these probably relate to the winter dances and may, for example, represent Bakbakwalanooksiwae in human form. Other series of

29. Northern Kwakiutl human face mask. Although the basic form of the mask is human, this almost certainly represents a character endowed with supernatural qualities. The human features have been broadened and flattened to produce a grotesque effect heightened by the superb asymmetrical facial painting. The eyes are movable and would have been manipulated by the dancer. *c. 1825–75. Height 9½in (24cm). Ipswich, Museum: DLJ 26.1976*

30. Northern Kwakiutl mask representing a spirit which, like many others, was collected from the grave of a shaman or man of high rank. The weathering has softened the features and removed most of the facial paint; the original impact of the mask would have been far stronger. *c. 1850–1900. Height 8in (20·5cm). Vancouver, Centennial Museum: AA 123*

human face masks were created by the Kwakiutl for minor characters in these performances, but their significance is also unrecorded.

The war-like nature of many of the songs used in the winter ceremonies suggests that the great growth of these performances during the first half of the nineteenth century is linked to a parallel decline in war. With the coming of Europeans and the slow elimination of actual fighting, competition for prestige between chiefs became confined to the giving of potlatches with performances of the winter dances. During the 1890s the performances began to disappear, while potlatching by chiefs, accompanied by the ceremonial disposal of property, continued.

31. Haida human face mask. This mask, decorated with fur, is very similar to that reproduced in plate 27; both may have been carved by the same artist under Kwakiutl influence. *c. 1880. Height 11⅜in (29cm). Berlin, Museum für Völkerkunde: 1V A 2473*

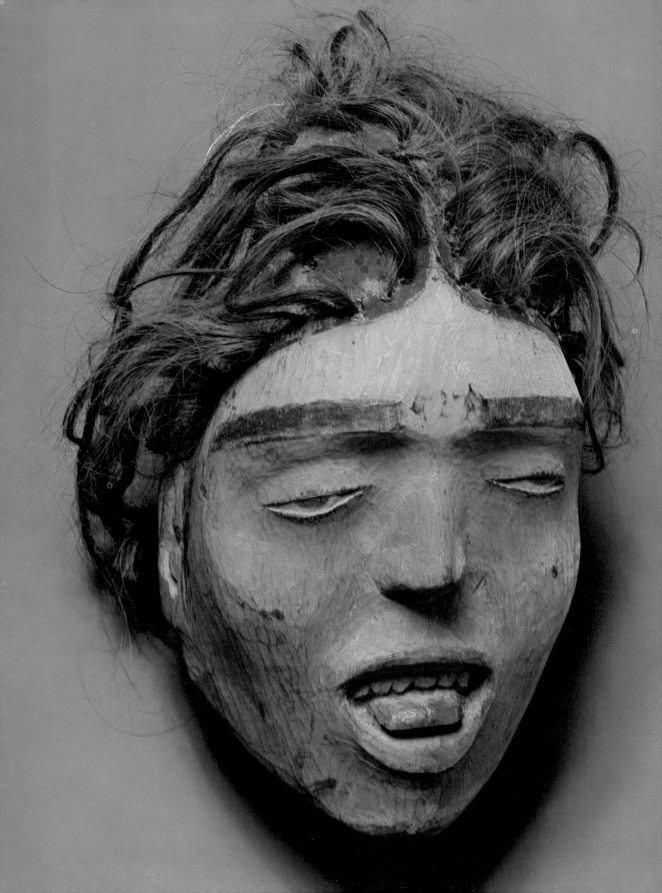

Nootkan Masks

There were two important moments of Nootkan rituals in which masks were used: the first was in the Shaman's Dance and the second was during potlatches. The Shaman's Dance was related to a similar series of performances among the Kwakiutl. The main part consisted of the ritual enactment of the seizure of a novice by a wolf and the bestowal on him of ancestral rights and powers. In this way novices were introduced to the ritual and rights of their family and village. The dancing and ceremonies lasted several days during which different groups of dancers performed imitations of natural phenomena, animals and people. Generally divided according to age, there might be seven such groups, three of men, three of women and one of war chiefs. The subjects of the dances were related to the property rights of chiefs, and were taken from the environment of the village. In one chief's house dancers would mimic the cormorant by imitating the motion of its wingbeat and throwing flour behind them to represent the cormorant's droppings. In another village dancers would imitate the black bear or land otter. Sometimes they wore masks, but more often they did not.

Another important occasion on which masks were worn was the announcing of potlatches. The announcement was made up to two years in advance so that chiefs in other villages would not organize feasts on conflicting dates. One method of announcing such a forthcoming event was to send guests stone crystals known as supernatural crystals because they were endowed with supernatural qualities. Alternatively the announcement was made by using two human face masks representing ancestors. At a minor feast arranged for this purpose the chief responsible for giving the major feast sent two people into the house wearing the masks of a male and a female ancestor. They entered the house and announced themselves by name through a speaker as ancestors of the chief. They described a feast they had given in the past and asked the chief whether he was able to give one of similar splendour in order to uphold the family name. The chief consulted his guests and then announced that he would try and provide a fitting ceremony at a particular time. All the details were arranged beforehand, but, of course, only a chief who owned the correct type of masks could announce a feast in this way.

Nootkan masks are unlikely to have been portraits, and would probably have merely represented ancestors in general ways. A more likely occasion for the use of portraiture would have been in the dramatizations which were a feature of the potlatch following the initiation of novices. These dramatizations, and the equipment that went with them, were owned by chiefs, who were privileged

32. Kwakiutl portrait carving of a woman performing the Toogwid dance. Both this one and plate 33 were collected by J. A. Jacobsen between 1881 and 1883 from one of the Kwakiutl groups on the northwest corner of Vancouver Island. The bold strokes, made by adzing, are still clearly visible. This mask and that in plate 33 are examples of Kwakiutl carving in the Nootkan style. *c. 1870–80. Height 11in (28cm). Berlin, Museum für Völkerkunde: 1V A 1348*

to use them as means of entertainment and of emphasizing their own wealth and power. A chief at the village of Kyuquot on northern Vancouver Island had the rights to the following masks: a Thunderbird which rose from the floor and flew across the room while the chief made his speeches; a supernatural canoe which moved across the house, suspended in the air from the roof; a bird monster with the body of a bear and a huge beak which snapped at small passing birds; a large human face mask which opened up to reveal rays around the face and so represented the sun. These dramatizations varied from chief to chief and from village to village and provided the context for a limited amount of portraiture.

Some of the finest Nootkan masks were collected in the eighteenth century by Spanish and English explorers; the significance of these masks is much less understood than those which were collected from the 1880s onwards by anthropologists. Captain James Cook collected a number of human face masks of which at least six have survived (plates 35, 36, 37, 38, 40); throughout the period that his sailors spent in Nootka Sound large numbers of artifacts were acquired but mostly without having been observed in use. On the second day after Cook's arrival the ships were surrounded by canoes in one of which a chief performed a dance using two masks. David Samwell, the surgeon's second mate, described the event in detail: '. . . the only performer appeared in a Mask, which was made of wood not badly carved & painted in the manner they generally do their faces, of these he had two expressing different Countenances which he changed every now & then; over his body was thrown a fine large wolfe Skin with the Hair outwards and a neat border worked round the edges of it; thus accoutred he jumped up and down in his Canoe with his arms extended, he moved his head different ways and shaked his fingers briskly, while he was acting in this manner all the other Indians sat down in their Canoes & sung in concert & struck the sides of their Canoes with the but end of their Paddles keeping exact time; every now & then the Concert wou'd cease and only an old woman in the same Canoe with the Performer was to be heard who made a bauling noise very much like some of the Cries of London.'(3)

This account gives an impressionistic if distorted picture of one use of human face masks; it does not explain why the performer was dancing. Two explanations have been offered; one is that the dancer, wearing a wolf skin, which would connect him to the role of the wolf in the Shaman's Dance, was calling on two spirits, represented by the two masks, to help him. The other is that the dancer was performing a potlatch welcome ceremony. Europeans had perhaps never been seen by Nootkans before, and since they

33. Kwakiutl portrait carving, similar in style to Nootkan masks (plates 34, 35, 36). The Kwakiutl used this type of carving in the Toogwid dance performed during the winter. In the darkened house, lit only by a fire, the spectators saw the dancer suddenly beheaded, and her head roll to the floor. These heads are bold and simple, the impassive features conveying a strong impression of a dead woman. *c. 1870–80. Height 10$\frac{1}{2}$in (27cm). Berlin, Museum für Völkerkunde: 1V A 1349*

34. Nootkan carving of a human head. This realistic carving of the head of a dead person may be one of those acquired by Captain Cook on 22 March 1778 when he persuaded some Indians to visit his cabin. Because of the stylistic similarities to carvings in plates 32 and 33 it may be associated with the Kwakiutl Toogwid dance. *c. 1750–75. Height 12$\frac{1}{2}$in (32cm). London, British Museum: NWC 58*

35. Nootkan human face mask probably collected by Captain Cook. *c. 1750–75. Florence, Museo Etnografico: 176*

37. Nootkan human face mask. Captain Cook collected this mask in 1778, together with those reproduced in plates 35, 36, 38, 40. *c. 1750–75. Height 8in (20·7cm). Vienna, Museum für Völkerkunde: 223*

36. Nootkan human face mask. This mask was collected by Captain Cook in 1778; it is characteristically Nootkan, in both the absence of paint and the use of decorative details. The human hair is pegged into the head, the eyes are made of mica stuck on to the mask with pine pitch, and the teeth are formed of split bird quills tied together with a length of twined hide. *c. 1750–75. Height $10\frac{1}{2}$in (27cm). London, British Museum: NWC 57*

38. Nootkan human face mask (?). Although it has the form
of a mask, it may not have been worn, since there is no
way in which the user could have seen where he was going.
The teeth, unlike those in plate 36, are made of small pieces
of bone instead of bird quill. *c. 1750–75. Height 11in (28cm).
London, British Museum: NWC 56*

39. Nootkan human face mask. The monstrous look of this
mask suggests that it represents a mythical character with
hideous – and perhaps cannibalistic – tendencies. The
carving, although simple, is typical of Nootkan sculpture; the
teeth are made of small pieces of wood. It was collected from
the Nootka or Makah during the 1840s. *c. 1840–50. Height
11in (28cm). London, British Museum: 50.6-3.1*

40. Nootkan human face mask. This is one of the few painted human face masks collected by Captain Cook, although the dark green abstract forms on the face are no longer visible. Cook appreciated the skills of the Nootkan carver, but did not suggest that these masks were portraits. *c. 1750–75. Height 10¼in (26cm). Houston, de Menil Collection*

41. *(Far left)* Nootkan human face mask. Both this and the mask in plate 40 resemble a mythical giantess of the Kwakiutl winter dances called Tsonokwa who was said to eat children. It may be that the idea of this person – or perhaps just the stylized form of the face – was borrowed by the Nootka. This mask is surmounted by a frontlet, perhaps of a frog or sea monster. *c. 1770–90. Madrid, Museo de America: 3309*

42. *(Left)* Tlingit (?) human face mask. This mask was collected in 1791 by Alejandro Malaspina from Yakutat in Alaska. However, the carving of the eyes and the application of fur for the eyebrows, moustache and beard suggest that it may be from further south. If it is Tlingit, the similarity of this mask to eighteenth-century Nootkan masks links it to an earlier common culture. *c. 1770–90. Height 8½in (22cm). Madrid, Museo de America: 1309*

appeared to be rich and powerful, they were obviously people to be invited to a ceremonial feast. If the second explanation is correct, then the masks worn may represent ancestors. However, none of the masks collected by Cook has been definitely identified with specific events recorded in the journals left by him and his men.

43. Nootkan human face mask. It is typical of late-nineteenth-century Nootkan masks with heavily exaggerated features and abstract painted designs, well outside northern formline traditions. *c. 1890–1900. Height 15½in (39·5cm). Victoria, British Columbia Provincial Museum: 10244*

Haida Masks

44. Haida portrait mask probably representing a middle-aged Haida woman, as indicated by the fullness of the cheeks — or perhaps a foreigner. Although the details of the face are different from others carved at approximately the same time, the structure of the face — and particularly of the eyes and nose — suggests that this was made by the same artist as those in plates 64 and 65. The eyes are movable. *c. 1870–1900. Berkeley, Lowie Museum of Anthropology: 2-15549*

Masks and human face masks were worn by chiefs and people of high rank at Haida potlatches. In general the masks of chiefs — although few have been specifically identified as such — were decorated with crests. The crests, of which more than fifty were recorded at the beginning of this century, represent such natural phenomena and animals as, for example, the new moon, killer whale, cirrus cloud, beaver and many others. Crests either harked back to the mythological past, or else, like many other aspects of Haida ceremonialism, were acquired from the Tsimshian. The Dog-Fish crest probably originated in the belief either that an ancestor was the first person to find a dog-fish, or that an ancestor, having displeased the Dog-Fish-House-People, was carried away by them. Crests as well as being depicted on masks and in facial

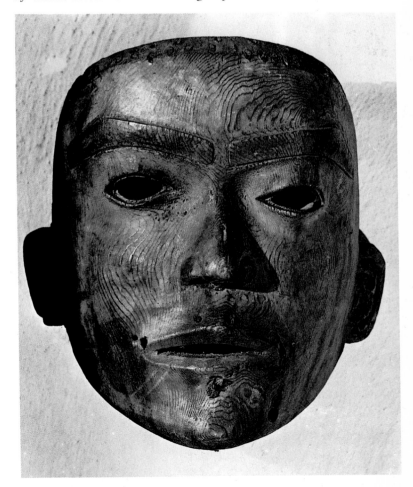

45. Haida (?) mask of a man. The eyelids are carved with unusual realism. *c. 1800–50. Height 9in (23cm). Leningrad, Museum of Anthropology and Ethnography: 5795-31*

46. Haida mask of a woman wearing a labret. The carving is
very similar to that of the other masks in this series; the
painting is unusual in that it is almost all green. This mask
was collected by Surgeon J. Neilson in the middle of the
nineteenth century. *c. 1825–50. Height 9½in (24cm). London.
British Museum: 55.17-20.195*

47. Haida human face mask. This is one of the few masks by
the same carver of the early group of Haida portraits which
does not show a woman with a labret. It may represent
either a young woman or a man. *c. 1825–50. Height* $9\frac{1}{2}$*in
(24cm). Ipswich, Museum: DLJ 25.1976*

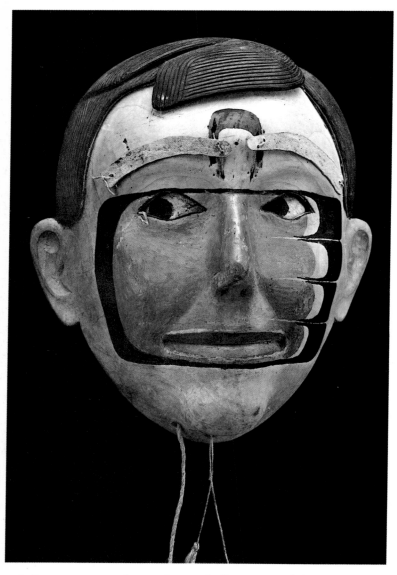

48. Haida portrait mask. This extremely effective mask is made of alder and painted red and black; the eyes are movable. *c. 1880–1900. Height $9\frac{1}{2}$in (24cm). Victoria, British Columbia Provincial Museum: 10655*

painting were carved, together with the stories of their origin, on house poles, and carved and painted on boxes, spoons, ladles and headdresses amongst other things. Large numbers of crests were owned by house chiefs, and even more by village chiefs.

A house chief headed the extended family which lived in one of the houses which went to make up a Haida village. Villages – the geographical expression of lineages which were the largest political

49. Haida human face mask, very finely carved with a minimum of facial painting. It is made of wood, and fur, probably glued on with pitch or gum from pine trees, has been added to the head and face to indicate hair, moustache and beard. It was collected, with those in plates 52 and 53, by Lieutenant Charles Wilkes. *c. 1841. Height $9\frac{1}{2}$in (24cm). Washington DC, Smithsonian Institution: 2658*

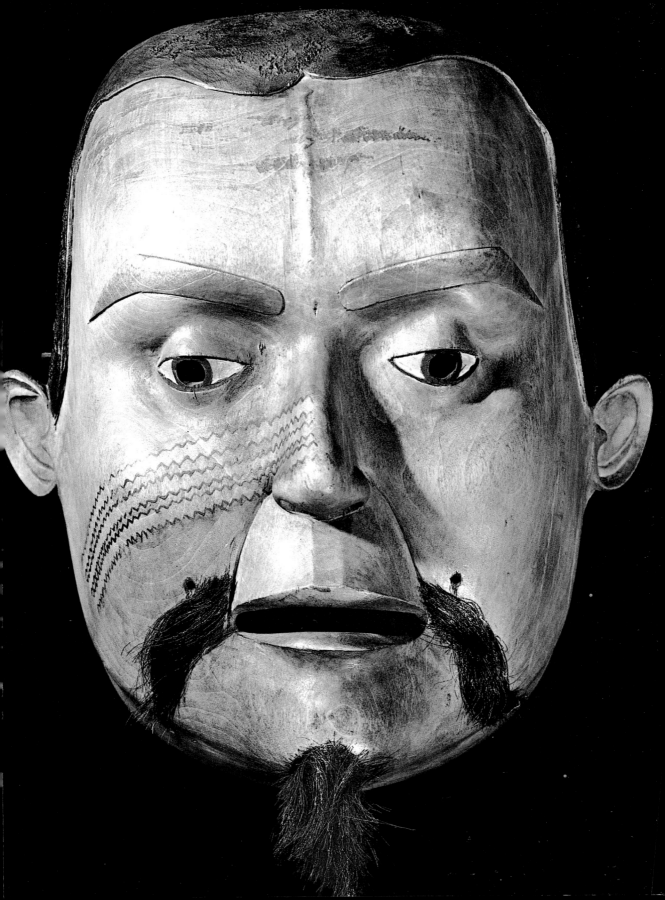

50. Haida mask of a woman wearing a labret. The eyes were originally inlaid with opaque blue glass beads of the type which the Russians probably first introduced to the Northwest Coast. The crest markings on the face are similar to those in plate 57, although the colours are different. *c. 1825–50. Height 8½in (23cm). Philadelphia, University Museum: 45-15-2*

51. Haida mask of a woman wearing a labret, the only example in the series which is definitely known to be a portrait. It was collected by J. Goodwin in 1826, and has inscribed on the back – presumably by Goodwin – 'A correct likeness of Jenna Cass, a high chief woman of the North west Coast J. Goodwin Esq.' *c. 1826. Height 10in (25·4cm). Cambridge, Mass., Peabody Museum (Harvard University): 10-47-10/76826*

units in Haida society — were headed by a village chief who was the house chief of the highest rank. It was these two groups of chiefs that gave potlatches and feasts and wore masks adorned with their crests. At the feasts food was distributed to previously invited guests arranged in the house in strict order of rank. Potlatches, given for example to commemorate an ancestor, the tattooing of a crest on a child or the cutting of a lip for a labret, were highly developed forms of feasts. The huge outlay of capital meant that chiefs had to borrow property from the other members of their family; part of this was paid back during the potlatch, by ritual services such as the tattooing of children of that family with their crests. Dances, derived from the Coast Tsimshian or Northern Kwakiutl in the seventeenth or eighteenth centuries, were also performed at an important event such as the setting up of a house pole. The characters and central ideas were similar to those elsewhere: the initiate into the group was possessed by a cannibal spirit and ran amok amongst the guests, frequently biting them. The host would then be obliged to rip up blankets — a sign of wealth

52. Haida (?) mask of a woman wearing a labret. This mask was collected with that reproduced in plate 53 and was probably carved by the same person. An inscription on the forehead, however, says that it came from near Fort Simpson in Tsimshian territory. *c. 1825–50. Height 9½in (24cm). Washington DC, Smithsonian Institution: 2665*

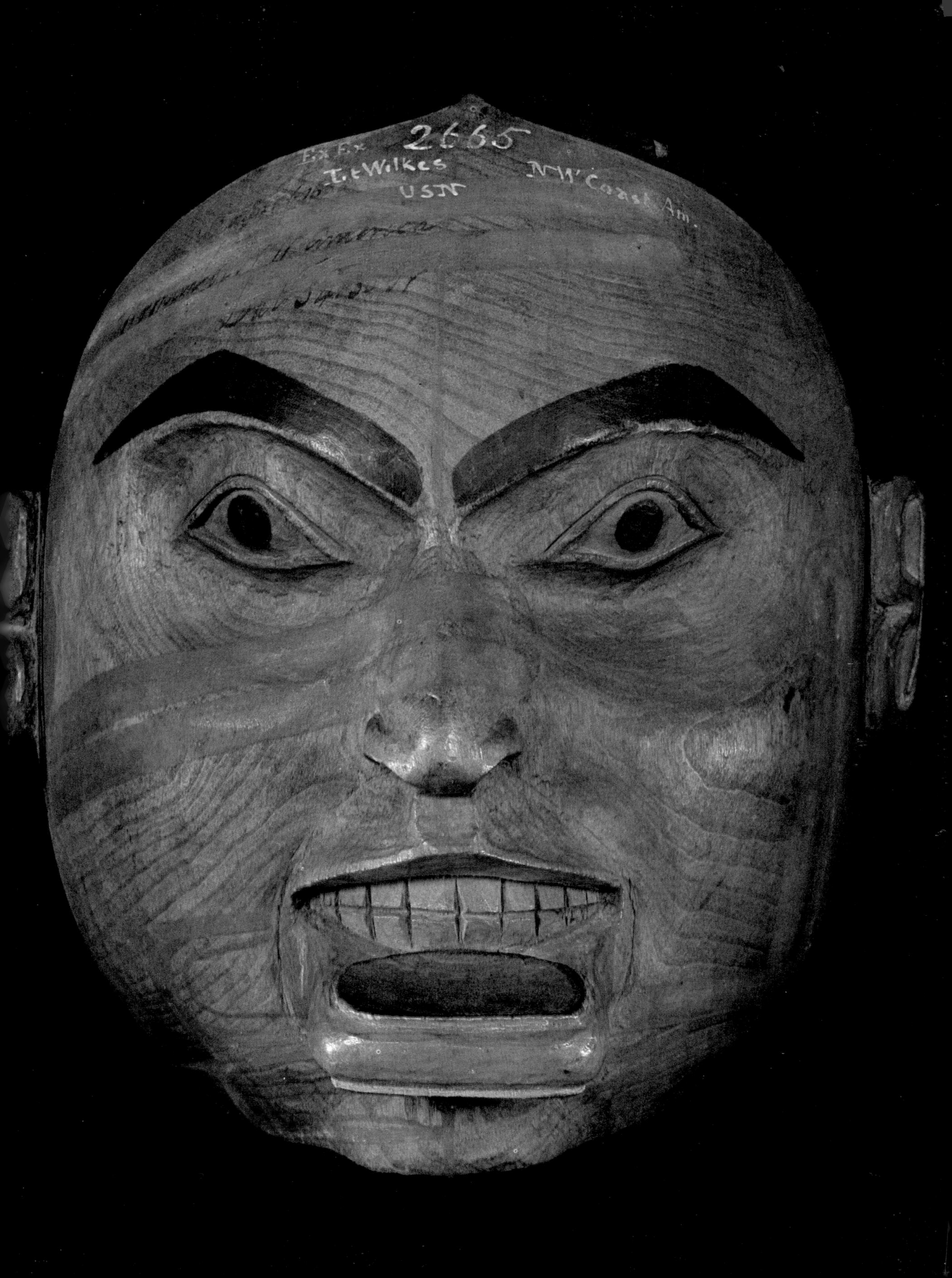
2665
Lt Wilkes
USN
NW Coast Am.

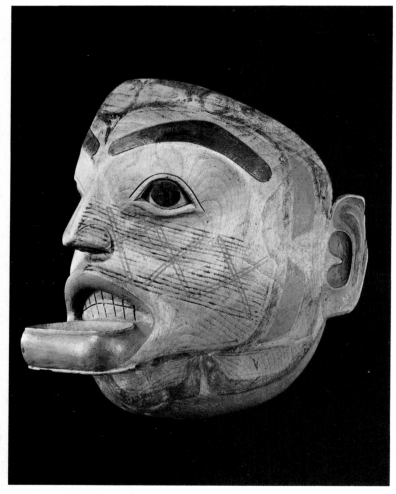

53a, 53b. Haida mask of a woman wearing
a labret. The red, green and black facial
painting is not repeated on any others of
this group (plates 13, 46, 47, 50, 51, 52,
56, 57, 58). This mask was collected by
Lieutenant Charles Wilkes on the United
States Exploring Expedition of 1838–42,
from fur traders at the mouth of the
Columbia River. *c. 1825–50. Height
7½in (19cm). Washington DC, Smithsonian
Institution: 2666*

and power – in order symbolically to wrap the wounds of those who
had been bitten by the cannibal spirit. These performances, of which
others included the Dog-Eating Spirit and the Grizzly Bear Spirit,
could only be danced on certain occasions because the spirits could
not be expected to appear simply at the convenience of the chief.
These dances were less important amongst the Haida than amongst
the Tsimshian.

A chief's prestige depended in part on the giving of successful
potlatches which in turn depended on the acquisition of wealth.
Extensive trade networks existed before the arrival of Europeans;
the Haida, for instance, traded dug-out canoes and carved boxes to
the Tsimshian in return for eulachon oil which they could not

54. Haida portrait mask of a woman with a labret. The quality of the carving and painting is not extraordinary, but the composition and the relationship of the features to each other make this one of the most expressive of all masks. The lower jaw moves so that the wearer could manipulate it as she spoke or danced. *c. 1825–70. Height 8¼in (21·6cm). Houston, de Menil Collection*

55. Haida portrait mask of a young woman. This exciting mask has movable eyes and the carved hair typical of many Haida masks; the mouth and lower half of the face are more Tsimshian in style. *c. 1825–75. Height 10½in (26·7cm). Rotterdam, Museum voor Land- en Volkenkunde: 34789*

56. Haida mask of a woman wearing a labret. *c. 1825–50. Height 9in (23cm). Rotterdam, Museum voor Land- en Volkenkunde: 34796*

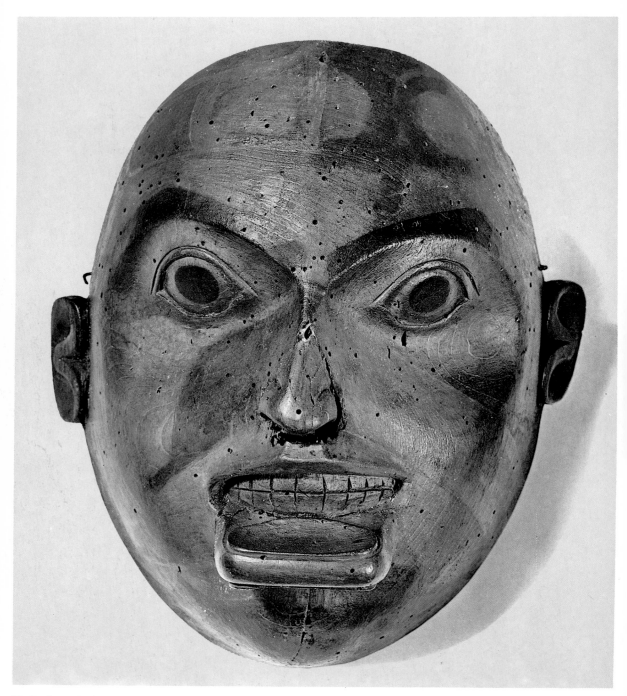

57. Haida mask of a woman wearing a labret. The abstract facial painting is almost identical to that in plate 13, except that this has an additional diagonal streak across the left cheek. *c. 1825–50. Height 9in (23cm). Ipswich, Museum: DLJ 24.1976*

58. Haida mask of a woman wearing a labret. It is peculiar in that it is very dirty and apparently coated in some kind of oil. This softens the rather uneven quality of the carving which is similar to that in plate 56. The strange surface is not necessarily an indication of much use, but may be the result of misuse in non-Indian hands during the nineteenth century. *c. 1825–50. Height 9¼in (23·5cm). Houston, de Menil Collection*

60. Portrait mask of a European or American. The facial features have been carved rather more carefully than those in plate 59; the staring look of the eyes may be meant to signify surprise or fear. *c. 1875–1900. Height 12¼in (31·25cm). Denver, Denver Art Museum: NHi-2*

59. Haida portrait mask of a European or American. The purpose of this type of mask is even less clear than it is for those of Haida men and women. It seems most likely that this too was carved for sale. The man has been given lavish stylized hair and what might be freckles of inlaid mirror with much the same effect as inlaid abalone shell. *c. 1850–1900. Height 10½in (26·75cm). Omaha, Joslyn Art Museum: 1959.532*

obtain on the Queen Charlotte's Islands. In the nineteenth century, after the sea otter had all but disappeared, the Haida found other goods to trade both to non-Indians and to the Tsimshian, including potatoes and their own artifacts. The first comparatively large-scale production of souvenirs was that of tobacco pipes carved of a shale known as argillite; although the Haida did not smoke before Europeans arrived, they subsequently carved pipes either in a traditional style with crests and mythological subjects, or else

61. *(Left)* Haida mask of a woman wearing a labret. The variations in the mouths of the faces painted on one side of this mask suggest that they represent a series of different crests or spirits. *c. 1825–75. Height 9⅛in (23·5cm). London, Wellcome Museum: 8793/1936*

63. *(Right)* Tlingit or Haida mask of a woman wearing a labret. The shape of the labret and the carving of the lips place this mask in the same tradition as the early series of Haida portrait masks. If, however, it is Haida, it is unusual in being painted with an overall design. It was collected in 1837. *c. 1837. Height 8in (20·5cm). Berlin, Museum für Völkerkunde: 1V B 34*

62. Two Haida masks of women. Neither of these two masks has been worn; it is probable that they were carved and painted for sale to missionaries or other collectors. The facial painting on the left-hand mask may represent a bird crest. Both were collected by the Reverend Dr Sheldon Jackson before 1882. *c. 1882. Princeton, Museum of Natural History: PU 3961 and 3924*

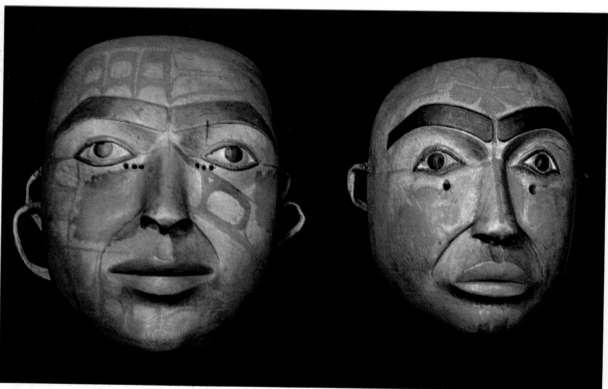

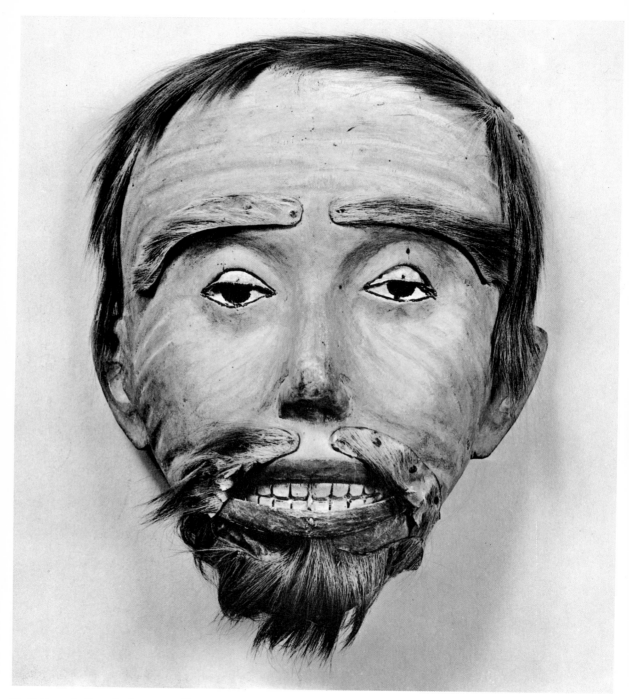

64. Haida portrait mask of a man. Unlike the mask in plate 65, which was carved by the same artist, this one has had fur added for hair as well as for eyebrows, moustache, and beard. *c. 1870–1900. Height 9in (23cm). Chicago, Field Museum of Natural History: 14262*

65. Haida portrait mask of a man. Said to come from Masset in the Queen Charlotte's Islands, this is one of a large group of portrait masks carved by the same artist towards the end of the nineteenth century (see plate 64). The masks of men often have stylized wrinkles on the cheeks and forehead, and sometimes have movable lips and eyebrows. *c. 1870–1900. Height 9¼in (23·75cm). Berkeley, Lowie Museum of Anthropology: 2-15550*

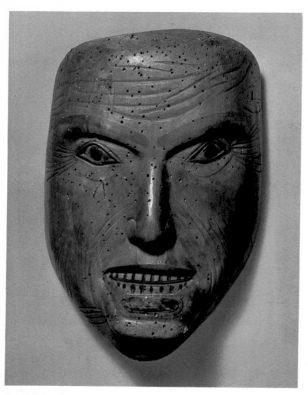

66. Haida portrait mask of a woman. This relatively simply carved mask belongs to the end of the Haida tradition of carving human representations. The labret is inlaid with abalone shell. *c. 1880–90. Height 9⅜in (24cm). London, British Museum: 1947 Am 5 3*

67. Haida portrait mask of a man. The expression of pain or surprise is unusual: Haida portrait masks are generally impassive. *c. 1880–90. Height 9⅜in (24cm). London, British Museum: 1947 Am 6 1*

represented European and American ships, people, houses and animals as part of a deliberate attempt to depict foreign subjects. One of the most common pipe forms of the 1830s shows a European sailor dressed in a tail-coat caught in the rigging of a ship; sometimes he is being chased by three bears carved in a more traditional style.

Very few objects, apart from pipes, were collected from the Haida before the 1860s and 1870s when, because of missionary activities and the ravages of smallpox, the structure of Indian society began to disintegrate. A few masks were collected in the first half of the nineteenth century, and most of these are human face masks; only one is said to be a portrait (plate 51), but many more may be thought of as such. There is a total of perhaps twenty or thirty, constituting only a minute proportion of Haida artistic output, ten of which are illustrated here (plates 13, 46, 47, 50, 51, 52, 53, 56, 57, 58). These masks, most often representing women of high rank wearing labrets and painted with abstract formline crest designs, were probably carved by one person between 1820 and 1840.

68. Haida portrait mask of a woman. This mask was collected in 1868 from a Haida carver portraying his wife. The collector, Dr F. Dally, noted that it was a very good likeness. Since it shows little or no signs of wear, it is unfortunate that he did not record whether it was made for ceremonial use or as a souvenir. The absence of the furrow under the nose has been taken as an indication of the carver's realistic treatment of the face: by distending the lower lip the effect of the labret was to draw the upper lip tightly across the teeth. As with other Haida masks of this date the wrinkled face of the woman is carved with great definition, but avoids the grotesque. *c. 1868. Oxford, Pitt-Rivers Museum*

There is no indication as to why this type of mask rather than any other should have been made for sale to Europeans. It may have been because traders liked and admired them, or it may be that the Haida were only prepared to carve and sell this type of mask because it had ceased to have any traditional significance. Other more valued ritual objects — for instance, shamans' regalia — only came to be depicted on souvenirs after the context for their use had ceased to exist. From the 1860s onwards several other series of portrait masks were produced (plates 64, 65, 69). They were more realistic than the earlier ones and were often produced in pairs of a man and a woman (plates 66 and 67, 70 and 71). Old age is frequently shown in the realistic carving of wrinkles, and hair is often added to represent men's facial hair. The meaning and purpose of these masks is even more mysterious than the earlier ones since they are seldom painted with crests.

69. Four Haida portrait masks, all probably carved by the same artist; he is identified in the museum records as Quaa-telth. The top left-hand mask, of a man, has parallel lines across the eye which represent the ribs of a bear and so form a bear crest. The marks on the forehead of the woman on the bottom right represent the killer whale crest. *c. 1870–1900. New York, American Museum of Natural History*

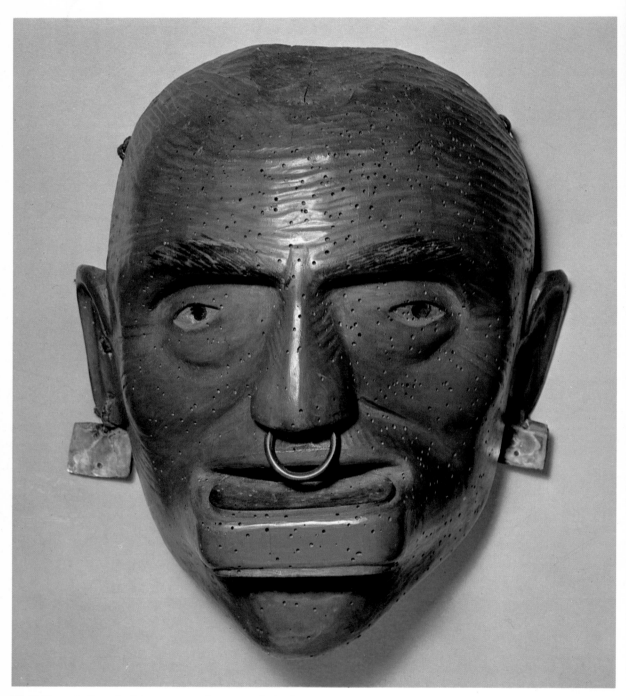

70. Haida portrait mask of a woman wearing ear pendants of abalone shell and a metal nose-ring. *c. 1880–90. Height $9\frac{3}{4}$in (25cm). London, British Museum: 1947 Am 5 1*

71. Haida portrait mask of a man. This type of mask, the pair to plate 70, was made for sale. These two and those in plates 65 and 67 were probably acquired by the Marquess of Lansdowne when he was Governor-General of Canada during the 1880s. The man has abalone shell earrings and a metal nose-ring. *c. 1880–90. Height $9\frac{3}{4}$in (25cm). London, British Museum: 1947 Am 5 2*

Tsimshian Masks

73. Tsimshian portrait mask of a woman. Two pendants in the form of birds are attached to the hair. *c. 1875–1900. Height 12in (30·8cm). Portland, Portland Art Museum: 46.14*

The Tsimshian used masks in much the same way as the Haida. Masks were worn at feasts given by chiefs, in ceremonies performed by shamans and in the performances of winter dances which were almost certainly acquired from the Northern Kwakiutl.

Tsimshian potlatches were given by chiefs to commemorate acquisition of powers and rights from lineage ancestors, the bestowal of rights on children, the erection of a new pole carved with crests, or the building of a new house. Potlatches were also given when chiefs' daughters first had their lips pierced for labrets and chiefs' sons first had their noses pierced for bone ornaments and feathers. As with other tribes the central theme was to display, by means of speeches, theatrical effects and dances, the wealth and importance of the chief giving the potlatch. Very few instances of portraiture have been authenticated amongst the paraphernalia associated with these Tsimshian feasts. Ancestral chiefs were carved on poles erected to commemorate them. The traditional ritual attached to these poles was very precise: if a pole decayed, refurbishment required a potlatch of a splendour and expense similar to that specified for the erection of a new one. There was therefore little incentive to carry out repairs when the same expenditure could produce a new pole. This may explain why Tsimshian carvings on poles often have standard features; even if portraiture had been a major element of Tsimshian representations of ancestors, in a very few generations the copying of old carvings would have led to the disappearance of the distinctive features of the person portrayed.

Theatre was an important part of Tsimshian potlatches, as it was of the Kwakiutl. One recorded use of portraiture occurred in a performance similar to that of the Kwakiutl Toogwid. In this dance the chief's uncle ran up to the dancer and cut off his head: it fell in a stream of blood near the fire. The shocked audience was quietened down and then the head was seen to dance round the fire — lit only by the firelight. This effect was achieved by means of a carved head with features resembling those of the chief. As with the Toogwid dance, the head was not intended to be a faithful and accurate portrait, but to convey a sense of the chief's features so that in the tense atmosphere it would be mistaken for a real head. The hair pegged into the head was, of course, the same colour as the chief's, and the head was made to dance (like a puppet) by means of strings worked from the roof. The blood was animal blood burst from a bladder. The performer danced crouching under a blanket so that his height did not give him away.

The craftsmen who created such effects were responsible for all aspects of their art. If there was any mechanical defect in the

72. Tsimshian mask of a man. This is an unusual mask because of the untraditional painting of chevrons and cross-hatching. *c. 1880–1910. Height 8⅝in (22cm). Los Angeles, Museum of Cultural History at UCLA: X 65-4273*

74. *(Above)* Tsimshian shaman's mask of a sea spirit. This mask, with whale features, illustrates how the stylized form of mammalian masks was adapted to incorporate features of other creatures. In this the face has been made long and narrow, the nose enlarged and, as in the Tlingit bear mask (plate 10), it has been given vertical ears. In general the shape of the eyes, nose and mouth is similar to that of a human face mask. The back of the mask is carved with five heads and a figure representing other spirits. *c. 1850–75. Length 21½in (55cm). Toronto, Royal Ontario Museum: 938.26.1*

77. *(Right)* Tsimshian or Tlingit human face mask. This mask, painted with what may be a crest design of a killer whale fin, has never been used. It was probably made specifically for sale, and was collected by Captain Sir Edward Belcher during the late 1830s. *c. 1835–40. Height 8¼in (21cm). London, British Museum: 42.12-10.84*

75. *(Far Left)* Tsimshian mask of a woman (?). Although very finely carved, this mask does not have the impact of many others of similar quality, because of the heaviness of the lower half of the face and partly because of the absence of facial painting. The hair-line is inlaid with abalone shell. *c. 1850–1900. Height 9in (22·9cm). Houston, de Menil Collection*

76. *(Left)* Tlingit (?) human face mask. Part of the lips has been broken off, but this mask seems to represent either a man with his tongue sticking out or a woman with a labret. *c. 1800–50. Height 8¼in (21cm). Leningrad, Museum of Anthropology and Ethnography: 2448-10*

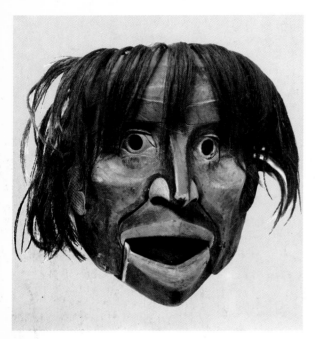

78. Tsimshian mask. Although this mask apparently represents a human being, the proportions of the face suggest that it may also have animal qualities. *c. 1825–75. Width 11in (28cm). New York, Heye Foundation*

79. Tsimshian human face mask. This fine early mask has a typical pentagonal Tsimshian shape, and is decorated with human hair pegged into the top. *c. 1800–50. Height 9in (23cm). New York, Heye Foundation: 3/4678*

performance – if a mask failed to open or if a deception failed to deceive – the craftsmen would be unable to pay compensation to the chief for the loss of face which it was felt he would have had to endure. Moreover, the craftsman responsible would be regarded as having lost his gift or touch and would not be asked to arrange any future performances. These men needed a very wide range of skills – not only did they have to be able to carve faithful representations of people, but they had to be able to achieve miraculous disappearances and reappearances. The greatest challenge to their craft would probably have been the initiation ceremonies when a novice was captured by a spirit and disappeared through the roof before returning with some magical device bestowed upon him by the spirit. Portraiture was, therefore, probably a small and relatively minor side of the craftsman's activities – a skill which he was expected to have, but not one to which special importance was attached.

80. Tlingit shaman's mask. The facial painting includes designs representing killer whale fins. The mask has two unusual features: the shaman's horn headdress is carved as an integral part of the mask and a whistle is inserted between the teeth at the left-hand side. *c. 1825–75. Height 12⅜in (31·5cm). Ipswich, Museum: DLJ 27.1976*

Tlingit Masks

Although the finest Tlingit representations of the human face are the masks used by shamans, the same quality of carving and decoration is apparent in the dance masks used in feasts and on clan and war helmets. At potlatches celebrating the memory of dead relatives, human face masks were worn and were decorated with the clan crests of relatives. They were worn by both men and women, the women's masks often carved with labrets. The piercing of the lip for these ornaments took place at the time of puberty. The facial painting on these masks, as with the other northern tribes, represented crests, heraldic badges or symbols of rank. The crests referred back to a mythological period when one of their deities, the Raven, provided the Tlingit with daylight.

Carved war helmets were made from large blocks of wood and designed both to terrify and to protect the wearer from wood and stone clubs and other weapons. In the eighteenth century they were worn with elaborate armour; an elk-hide tunic covered the body and on top of that wooden slat armour was bound together by sinew over the torso. The legs were protected by wooden slat greaves, and the lower half of the face by a circular piece of wood which was constructed from a straight piece of kerfing, or cutting out v-sections and steaming and bending into shape. The war helmets were carved with grotesque and fearsome representations of human or supernatural creatures with human attributes. It is possible that these helmets may occasionally have portrayed individuals, but there is no way of knowing this. Any such suggestions remain in the realm of conjecture, and largely depend on the non-Indian assessment of the quality of the carving.

Tlingit shamans owned and wore a large number of masks which were associated with and represented their spirit helpers. Although the shaman's position was inherited, together with the masks and regalia, nobody could become a shaman unless he had the understanding of or contact with the necessary spirits. Equally, some people could not avoid becoming shamans even though they had no wish to, because they were in contact with the spirits. Before becoming a shaman, a person, generally a man, would go into the mountains alone for a period of time and live off roots and other plants; eventually, if he were destined to become a shaman, he would meet and obtain the help of a spirit. The most powerful of these spirits was the land otter. For that reason, before the arrival of the Russians, no Tlingit, unless he was a shaman, would kill it. In the Tlingit cosmology (which differed slightly from that of the Haida) there were three kinds of spirits with whom the shamans were in contact: those of the upper world who lived in the heavens and were souls of dead warriors, the sea or water spirits or souls of

81. Tlingit shaman's mask of a drowned man who, like all drowned men, was believed to have turned into a land otter man. *c. 1850–80. Height $8\frac{1}{2}$ in (22cm). New York, American Museum of Natural History: E/400*

82. Tlingit shaman's mask representing the moon. The moon and many other natural phenomena were given human attributes in Tlingit masks. Here the round face appears flat; the eyes, nose and mouth are formalized and reduced in prominence to suggest the moon. This mask was collected in the Sitka neighbourhood and was presented with plate 87 to the Princeton Museum in 1882 by the Reverend Dr Sheldon Jackson. *c. 1840–70. Princeton, Museum of Natural History: PU 3912*

83. Tlingit mask of a woman wearing a labret. This mask was collected together with plate 4 during the 1860s. They were both probably carved by the same person, the most distinctive feature being the deep lines carved in the face between the nose and the corner of the mouth. *c. 1860–65. Height 9in (23cm). Moscow, Anthropological Museum of Lomonsov State University: 237-8*

84. Tlingit shaman's mask. The greenish pallor, grimace and wrinkles suggest that it represents the spirit of a man who was dead or dying. *c. 1850–1900. Height 8¼in (21cm). Salem, Peabody Museum: E 16700*

sea mammals and the souls of land animals. In addition, every Tlingit, whether a shaman or not, traditionally had his or her guardian spirit. The major role of the shamans was to call on their spirits, not only to bring good fortune to themselves, but also to the village where they and their relations lived. The most important of these ceremonies took place in winter at full moon; spirits appeared to the shaman who danced wearing the appropriate mask and costume. The chief's house would have been filled with people who would both sing and listen to the predictions of the shaman. He had two other subsidiary but important roles: the first was that of healer, the person who drove away the evil spirits, the second was that of exposing witches. Witches, of both sexes, did

87. **Tlingit mask representing a woman of high rank wearing a labret in her lower lip. It is, however, surprisingly decorated with hair along the lower neck.** *c. 1840–70. Height 9¼in (23·6cm). Princeton, Museum of Natural History: PU 3926*

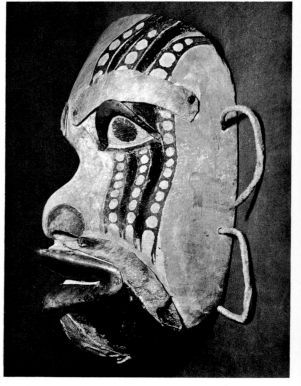

85. **Tlingit or Tsimshian human face mask. It is not clear whether this mask represents a man or woman. The eyes are carved in a Tsimshian manner, but the facial painting is more Tlingit in character.** *c. 1875–1900. Paris, Musée de l'Homme*

86. **Tlingit shaman's mask. The lips are decorated with copper and the face with two series of tattoos representing octopus tentacles. The moustache and eyebrows were originally of fur. Both this mask and that in plate 88 were collected by Professor William S. Libbey from a shaman's grave near Port Mulgrave, Yakutat, Alaska.** *c. 1825–75. Height 9¾in (24·7cm). Princeton, Museum of Natural History: PU 3923*

88. Tlingit shaman's mask. Although very different from the masks in plates 89 and 90, it may also be of a shaman singing. *c. 1825–75. Princeton, Museum of Natural History: PU 3957*

89. Tlingit shaman's mask, like plate 90, of a shaman singing. *c. 1800–50. Height 7⅝in (19·5cm). Leningrad, Museum of Anthropology and Ethnography: 5795-32*

90. Tlingit shaman's mask. The pursed lips represent a shaman singing, but the significance of the facial painting is obscure; however the broad nose suggests that the shaman's spirit may have been of mammalian form. *c. 1840–60. Height 9¼in (23·5cm). London, British Museum: St 705*

harm with the help of the raven, to those of whom they were jealous. This harm was done by taking a piece of hair or dirt from somebody and placing it with the necessary ritual near a body or remains of a corpse. The shaman would persuade or torture the witch until he or she confessed to the deed; the witch was either killed or died from the treatment received.

Much of a shaman's regalia was buried with him when he died, and it is from nineteenth-century graves that the finest of their objects have been collected. Shamans' bodies were never supposed to decay, but the coffins and posts on which they were placed were almost never touched. Shamanistic figures, carved with grotesquely realistic features, were placed by them to keep people away. If a spirit had not previously appeared to a prospective shaman, he might visit a shaman's grave and take a tooth, or some other part of a shaman's body, and place it in his mouth to help him make contact with spirits.

Shamans were not usually people of high birth and shamanism was a means of achieving high status and, to some extent, wealth. Shamans were in an entirely different position to chiefs, and were unable to challenge their status. Not only was it impossible for them to accumulate enough riches from payments for healing to give a potlatch, but also, unlike chiefs, they were unable to call on any family help in providing money. Shamans' masks were apparently different to those of chiefs and their lineages. Whereas chiefs commemorated ancestors with their masks, shamans became the agents of the supernatural phenomena by whose spirit they were possessed. These were portrayed in groups of masks representing a whole series of spirits, as, for example, sky spirits from the upper world. All Tlingit masks, and indeed all Northwest Coast masks, combine this aim of representing spirits and ancestors with an attempt to create impressive and instantly recognizable images. In achieving these ends, portrait masks express a talent which transcends the context of Indian society and enables them to take their place among the finest art of the world.

91. Tlingit (?) mask of a woman wearing a labret. The detailed carving of the teeth gives this woman a grotesque appearance. *c. 1825–75. Height 8½in (21·5cm). Leningrad, Museum of Anthropology and Ethnography: 337-2*

92. Tlingit mask. The grotesque lips suggest an element of caricature – the mask may represent an Athapascan from a neighbouring tribe. *c. 1825–75. Height 8½in (21·5cm). New York, Heye Foundation: 9/7984*

93. Tlingit (?) human face mask. Above the left eye is a killer whale fin and below the lower lip are two octopus tentacles; three other designs, on the cheeks and above the right eye, may represent other crests. *c. 1850–90. Height 9in (23cm). Moscow, Anthropological Museum of Lomonsov State University: 237-9*

94. Tlingit shaman's mask, an unusually expressive mask carved with much deeper features than was usual in Tlingit masks. As in plate 5, the face is decorated with hair and fur and copper lips, nostrils and eyebrows. It was collected on Admiralty Island, Alaska, by G. Chudnovsky in 1890. *c. 1870–90. Height 11in (28cm). Leningrad, Museum of Anthropology and Ethnography: 211-7*

95. Tlingit (?) shaman's mask. Tlingit masks and helmets are frequently adorned with inset hair (see the helmet in plate 19). *c. 1850–60. Height 11in (28cm). Cambridge, Mass., Peabody Museum (Harvard University): 69-30-10/1699*

Notes

1. Franz Boas, *The Social Organization and the Secret Societies of the Kwakiutl Indians*, p. 476
2. Ibid., p. 471

3. J. C. Beaglehole, *The Voyage of the* Resolution *and the* Discovery *1776–1780*, Cambridge 1967, pp. 1089–90

Bibliography

General books about the Indians of the Northwest Coast:
Drucker, Philip: *Indians of the Northwest Coast*. Garden City, The Natural History Press, New York, 1963
Gunther, Erna: *Indian Life on the Northwest Coast of North America*. University of Chicago Press, Chicago, 1972
Niblack, Albert P.: 'The Coast Indians of southern Alaska and northern British Columbia', in the *Annual Report of the Board of Regents of the Smithsonian Institution for 1888*, Washington DC, 1890

General books about the art of the Northwest Coast:
Boas, Franz: *Primitive Art*. Dover, New York, 1955
Hawthorn, Audrey: *Art of the Kwakiutl Indians*. University of British Columbia Press, Vancouver, 1967
Holm, Bill: *Northwest Coast Indian Art*. University of Washington Press, Seattle, 1965
Holm, Bill, and Reid, William: *Form and Freedom*. Rice University, Houston, 1975
Wingert, Paul S.: 'Tsimshian Sculpture' in *The Tsimshian, their Arts and Music* (ed. Viola E. Garfield), J. J. Augustin, New York, 1951

Publications discussing Northwest Coast masks:
Balfour, Henry: *Haida Portrait Mask*, in *Man*, Volume VII, London 1907
Boas, Franz: *The Use of Masks and Head-ornaments on the Northwest Coast of America*, in *Internationales Archiv für Ethnographie*, Volume III, Leiden, 1890
Emmons, G. T.: 'Portraiture among the North Pacific Coast Tribes', in *American Anthropologist*, new series, Volume 16, Washington DC, 1914

Lévi-Strauss, Claude: *La voie des masques*. Albert Skira, Geneva, 1975
Mochon, Marion Johnson: *Masks of the Northwest Coast*, in *Primitive Art 2*, Milwaukee Public Museum, 1966
Malin, Edward: *A World of Faces*. Timber Press, Portland, 1978
Holm, Bill: *Crooked Beak of Heaven*. University of Washington Press, Seattle, 1972

Ethnographical accounts of Northwest Coast tribes:
Boas, Franz: 'The Social Organization and the Secret Societies of the Kwakiutl Indians', in the *Annual Report of the Board of Regents of the Smithsonian Institution for 1895*, Washington DC, 1897
Boas, Franz: 'The Kwakiutl of Vancouver Island', in the *Jesup North Pacific Expedition*, Volume V, part 2. American Museum of Natural History, New York, 1909
Drucker, Philip: 'The Northern and Central Nootkan Tribes', in *The Smithsonian Institution Bureau of Ethnology Bulletin 144*, Washington DC, 1951
Garfield, Viola E.: *Tsimshian Clan and Society*. University of Washington, Seattle, 1939
Krause, Aurel: *The Tlingit Indians*. University of Washington Press, Seattle, 1956
Laguna, Frederica de: *Under Mount Saint Elias: The History and Culture of the Yakutat Tlingit*, Parts I–III. Smithsonian Contributions to Anthropology, Washington DC, 1972
Swanton, John R.: 'Contributions to the Ethnology of the Haida', in the *Jesup North Pacific Expedition*, Volume V, part I. American Museum of Natural History, New York, 1905

Acknowledgements and list of illustrations

The author would like to thank Bill Holm for his advice on the text and Dr Edmund Carpenter for his help in the selection of the illustrations. The author and Blacker Calmann Cooper Ltd would like to thank the museums who allowed works in their collections to be reproduced in this book. Unless otherwise stated they provided the photographs from which the illustrations were made.

1. Haida village of Skidegate. American Museum of Natural History, New York
2. Haida or Northern Kwakiutl human face mask. Ulster Museum, Belfast
3. The inside of a house in Nootka Sound
4. Tlingit mask of a woman wearing a labret. Peabody Museum (Harvard University), Cambridge, Mass. Photo Hillel Burger
5. Tlingit shaman's mask. Smithsonian Institution, Washington DC

6. Medicine Mask dance by Paul Kane. Royal Ontario Museum, Toronto
7. Haida figure of a shaman. Courtesy of the Trustees of the British Museum, London
8. Northern Kwakiutl mask. Courtesy of the Trustees of the British Museum, London
9. Interior of a Kwakiutl house before a potlatch. American Museum of Natural History, New York
10. Tlingit shaman's mask in the form of a bear. Peabody Museum (Harvard University), Cambridge, Mass. Photo Hillel Burger
11. Tsimshian chiefs with heirlooms. Museum of Northern British Columbia, Prince Rupert
12. Haida mask of a dead man. Museum für Völkerkunde, Berlin
13. Haida mask of a woman wearing a labret. Peabody Museum, Salem

14. Portrait bust of Captain Reid. Courtesy of the Trustees of the British Museum, London
15. Haida mask of a man. De Menil Collection, Houston
16. Haida mask of a man. Courtesy of the Trustees of the British Museum, London
17. Four Haida. American Museum of Natural History, New York
18. Haida mask of a man. Smithsonian Institution, Washington DC
19. Tlingit war helmet. Museum of Anthropology and Ethnography, Leningrad (photo Werner Forman Archive)
20. Woman's labret. Courtesy of the Trustees of the British Museum, London
21. Tsimshian human face mask. De Menil Collection, Houston
22. Northern Kwakiutl mask of a man. Ipswich Museum, Ipswich
23. Northern Kwakiutl mask of a man. Courtesy of the Trustees of the British Museum, London
24. Northern Kwakiutl mask of a man. Peabody Museum, Salem
25. Northern Kwakiutl mask of a man. Smithsonian Institution, Washington DC
26. Kwakiutl mask representing Noohlmahl. Ipswich Museum, Ipswich
27. Haida mask of a woman. De Menil Collection, Houston
28. Kwakiutl human face mask. Ipswich Museum, Ipswich
29. Northern Kwakiutl human face mask. Ipswich Museum, Ipswich
30. Northern Kwakiutl mask. Centennial Museum, Vancouver
31. Haida human face mask. Museum für Völkerkunde, Berlin
32. Kwakiutl portrait carving. Museum für Völkerkunde, Berlin
33. Kwakiutl carving. Museum für Völkerkunde, Berlin
34. Nootkan carving of a human head. Courtesy of the Trustees of the British Museum, London
35. Nootkan human face mask. Museo Etnografico, Florence
36. Nootkan human face mask. Courtesy of the Trustees of the British Museum, London
37. Nootkan human face mask. Museum für Völkerkunde, Vienna
38. Nootkan human face mask. Courtesy of the Trustees of the British Museum, London
39. Nootkan human face mask. Courtesy of the Trustees of the British Museum, London
40. Nootkan human face mask. De Menil Collection, Houston
41. Nootkan human face mask. Museo de America, Madrid. Photo Museum of New Mexico
42. Tlingit (?) human face mask. Museo de America, Madrid. Photo Museum of New Mexico
43. Nootkan human face mask. British Columbia Provincial Museum
44. Haida portrait mask of a woman. Lowie Museum of Anthropology, University of California, Berkeley
45. Haida (?) mask of a man. Museum of Anthropology and Ethnography, Leningrad. Photo Werner Forman Archive
46. Haida mask of a woman wearing a labret. Courtesy of the Trustees of the British Museum, London
47. Haida human face mask. Ipswich Museum, Ipswich
48. Haida portrait mask. British Columbia Provincial Museum
49. Haida human face mask. Smithsonian Institution, Washington DC
50. Haida mask of a woman wearing a labret. University Museum, Philadelphia
51. Haida mask of a woman wearing a labret. Peabody Museum (Harvard University), Cambridge, Mass. Photo Hillel Burger
52. Haida (?) mask of a woman wearing a labret. Smithsonian Institution, Washington DC
53 a & b. Haida mask of a woman wearing a labret. Smithsonian Institution, Washington DC
54. Haida portrait mask of a woman with labret. De Menil Collection, Houston
55. Haida portrait mask of a young woman. Museum voor Land- en Volkerkunde, Rotterdam
56. Haida mask of a woman wearing a labret. Museum voor Land- en Volkerkunde, Rotterdam
57. Haida mask of a woman wearing a labret. Ipswich Museum, Ipswich
58. Haida mask of a woman wearing a labret. De Menil Collection, Houston
59. Haida portrait mask of a European or American. Joslyn Museum, Omaha. Photo Werner Forman Archive
60. Portrait mask of a European or American. Denver Art Museum, Denver
61. Haida mask of a woman wearing a labret. Wellcome Institute, London. (By courtesy of the Wellcome Trustees)
62. Two Haida masks of women. Museum of Natural History, Princeton
63. Tlingit or Haida mask of a woman wearing a labret. Museum für Völkerkunde, Berlin
64. Haida portrait mask of a man. Field Museum of Natural History, Chicago
65. Haida portrait mask of a man. Lowie Museum of Anthropology, University of California, Berkeley
66. Haida portrait mask of a woman. Courtesy of the Trustees of the British Museum, London
67. Haida portrait mask of a man. Courtesy of the Trustees of the British Museum, London
68. Haida portrait mask of a woman. Pitt-Rivers Museum, Oxford
69. Four Haida portrait masks. American Museum of Natural History, New York
70. Haida portrait mask of a woman. Courtesy of the Trustees of the British Museum, London
71. Haida portrait mask of a man. Courtesy of the Trustees of the British Museum, London
72. Tsimshian mask of a man. Museum of Cultural History, Los Angeles
73. Tsimshian portrait mask of a woman. Portland Art Museum, Portland. Photo Werner Forman Archive
74. Tsimshian shaman's mask of a sea spirit. Royal Ontario Museum, Toronto
75. Tsimshian mask of a woman. De Menil Collection, Houston
76. Tlingit (?) human face mask. Museum of Anthropology, Leningrad. Photo Werner Forman Archive
77. Tsimshian or Tlingit human face mask. Courtesy of the Trustees of the British Museum, London
78. Tsimshian mask. Heye Foundation, New York
79. Tsimshian human face mask. Museum of the American Indian, Heye Foundation, New York
80. Tsimshian shaman's mask. Ipswich Museum, Ipswich
81. Tlingit shaman's mask. American Museum of Natural History, New York
82. Tlingit shaman's mask representing the moon. Museum of Natural History, Princeton
83. Tlingit mask of a woman wearing a labret. Anthropological Museum of Lomonsov State University, Moscow. Photo Werner Forman Archive
84. Tlingit shaman's mask. Peabody Museum, Salem
85. Tlingit or Tsimshian human face mask. Musée de l'Homme, Paris
86. Tlingit shaman's mask. Museum of Natural History, Princeton
87. Tlingit mask. Museum of Natural History, Princeton
88. Tlingit shaman's mask. Museum of Natural History, Princeton
89. Tlingit shaman's mask. Museum of Anthropology and Ethnography, Leningrad. Photo Werner Forman Archive
90. Tlingit shaman's mask. Courtesy of the Trustees of the British Museum, London
91. Tlingit (?) mask of a woman wearing a labret. Museum of Anthropology and Ethnography, Leningrad. Photo Werner Forman Archive
92. Tlingit mask. Museum of the American Indian, Heye Foundation, New York
93. Tlingit (?) human face mask. Anthropological Museum of Lomonsov State University, Moscow. Photo Werner Forman Archive
94. Tlingit shaman's mask. Museum of Anthropology and Ethnography, Leningrad. Photo Werner Forman Archive
95. Tlingit (?) shaman's mask. Peabody Museum (Harvard University), Cambridge, Mass. Photo Hillel Burger

Index

Page numbers in *italic* refer to illustrations

abstract design, 28–30
Alert Bay, 23
animals, symbolism, 28
animal crests, 13, 16, 31, 51–4
armour, 22, 83
art, Northwest Coast, 27–31

Bakbakwalanooksiwae, 33, 38
beavers, animal crests, 51; depiction, 28
bird masks, 27, 33
Boas, Franz, 27, 28, 33
Bookwus, *15*

cannibalism, 23, 33, 34–7
Catlin, George, 26
clans, 13
cod, as food, 6, 9
Cook, Captain James, 19, 23, 44–8
crests, animal, 13, 16, 31, 51–4

dances, 5; Haida, 56, 58; Kwakiutl, 33–40; Nootkan, 43–8; Tsimshian, 56, 58, 77
deities, 13–14
diseases, 22
dog-fish, animal crests, 51

Eagle moiety, 13

feasts, *see* potlatches
fish, 6–9, 14
food, 6–9; *see also* potlatches
Fort Astoria, 22
Fort Rupert, 23
Fort Vancouver, 26
Fort Victoria, 26
frog, animal crests, 13
fur trade, 19, 22

Haida, *26*; abstract designs, 30; carved details, 30; crests, 31; location, 6; masks, 29, 51–72; *7, 20, 21, 24–6, 38, 41, 50–75*; portrait masks, *50, 54, 60, 64, 65, 68–75*; potlatches, 18, 51, 56, 58; shaman, *14*; society and religion, 9–18; trade, 26, 58, 65
halibut, as food, 6, 9
Hamatsa, 33–4, 36
healing, 5

herring, as food, 6, 9
history, 19–27
Holm, Bill, 28
houses, *8, 16*
Hudson Bay Company, 22, 27
hunting, 6–9

Kane, Paul, 26; *12*
killer whales, *see* whales
Kwakiutl, carved details, 30; decorative designs, 30; location, 6; mask painting, 31; masks, 7, 33–40; *15, 34–40*; portrait carvings, *42, 44*; potlatches, 33, 40; *16*; society and religion, 9–18
Kyuquot, 44

labrets, 31; *31*; ceremonies concerning, 56, 77; in masks, 83; *4, 38, 52, 56–63, 70, 74, 84, 87, 91*
lineages, 12–13

Makah, hunting, 8
masks, art of, 27–31; carving, 30–1; facial painting, 31; significance, 27; trade in, 23–7, 70, 72
missionaries, 27
moieties, 13
moon, *84*

Noohlmahl, masks, 34–6; *37*
Nootka, clothing, 19; decorative designs, 30; descent, 12; houses, 8; hunting, 8; location, 6; masks, 43–8; *44–9*; potlatches, *44–9*; society and religion, 9–18; trade, 19, 23, 26; weapons, 19
Nootka Sound, 22
North West Company, 22

octopus, animal crests, 16; represented on masks, *86*

Pacific Fur Company, 22
patron spirits, 14
pipes, Haida, 65, 70
population, decline, 22–3
portrait busts, *23*
potlatches, 16–18, 23; Haida, 18, 51, 56, 58; Kwakiutl, 33, 40; *16*; Nootka, 43; Tlingit, 18, 83; Tsimshian, 18, 77
Power-of-the-Shining-Heavens, 14

Queen Charlotte's Islands, 6, 14

Raven-at-the-Mouth-of-the-Nass-River, 13
Raven deity, 83
Raven moieties, 13
ravens, animal crests, 13, 16
Reid, George, *23*
religion, 9–18

Sacred-One-Standing-and-Moving, 14
salmon, as food, 6, 9; myths associated with, 14
Samwell, David, 44
sea otters, fur trade, 19, 22, 26
shamans, 14, 83–91; dance, 43, 44; *12*; figure of, *14*; helper's mask, 7; masks, 5, 77, 83, 90; *11, 17, 78, 81, 84–6, 88–9, 92–3*; powers, 14; ritual, *12*; role, 84; sea spirit mask, *78*
Skidegate, 4
society, 9–18
songs, Kwakiutl, 40

Thunderbird, 33, 44
Tlingit, abstract designs, 30; carved details, 30; location, 6; masks, 83–90; *10, 11, 17, 48, 67, 78, 79, 82–95*; portrait busts, *23*; potlatches, 18, 83; shamanism, 31; society and religion, 9–18; war helmet, *30*; weapons, 22
tobacco pipes, 65, 70
Tsetseka, 33
Tsimshian, abstract designs, 30; chiefs, *18*; location, 6; masks, 77–80; *32, 76–81, 86*; portrait masks, 77, 80; *77*; potlatches, 18, 77; society and religion, 9–18; trade, 65
Tsonokwa, *48*

Vancouver Island, 8
villages, *4*

war helmets, 83
weapons, 19–22
whales, animal crests, 13, 16, 51; *73, 79, 80*; depicted on masks, *10*; as food, 8; as sea spirits, 14, 16; symbolism, 28
Wilkes, Charles, 26
Winalagilis, 36
Wingert, Paul, 28
wolf, masks, 27; Shaman's Dance, 44